Gems and Jewels

A Connoisseur's Guide

Gems and Jewels

A Connoisseur's Guide

BENJAMIN ZUCKER

For Jason —

WHEN you get MARRIED come
to me for A Ring and I hope I will
be able to MATCH the good service
your uncle and you are giving me —

Benjamin Zucker —

1212 819 0001 —

THE OVERLOOK PRESS
Woodstock & New York

To
LOTTY GUTWIRTH ZUCKER
(an inspiration to us all)
with thanks for the love
shown to me and to Rachel,
and to
CHARLES ZUCKER
with thanks for his energetic
and wholehearted encouragement

and ever and always
to my darling
BARBARA ZUCKER

This edition first published in the United States in 2003 by
The Overlook Press, Peter Mayer Publishers, Inc.
Woodstock & New York

WOODSTOCK:
One Overlook Drive
Woodstock, NY 12498
www.overlookpress.com
[for individual orders, bulk and special sales, contact our Woodstock office]

NEW YORK:
141 Wooster Street
New York, NY 10012

Cataloging-in-Publication Data is available from the Library of Congress.

Book design and type formatting by Bernard Schleifer
Manufactured in China
ISBN 1-58567-420-6
1 3 5 7 9 8 6 4 2

Contents

Introduction

WHY ARE GEMS so alluring? Ultimately, gems are alluring in the same way that humans are alluring. A man in love sees a woman as colorful, scintillating, brilliant, extraordinarily rare, exotic and overwhelmingly and mysteriously beautiful. A gem has exactly these qualities. It is not surprising, therefore, that down the ages gems have come to be tokens of the love and desire that a man feels for a woman. A woman instinctively knows that once she receives a gem as a gift it becomes a part of her mystery, and its loveliness, its brilliance and its colorfulness in a sense reflect her own charms.

Gems partake of the ultimate mystery of the world, light. Two thousand years ago, in India, gem merchants would hold up a pure octahedral diamond crystal to the light and demonstrate a remarkable phenomenon: "white" light would be split into its prismatic color spectrum—red, orange, yellow, green, blue, indigo and violet. To the extent that the diamond crystal was pure and perfectly colorless, the prismatic colors revealed on the surface of the gem dealer's wall would be clear and most intense. Thus, one can imagine the extraordinary fascination a perfectly formed diamond crystal would have had for a princely beholder. Diamonds were regarded as so extraordinary in their purest form that only Brahmins were allowed to purchase such flawless uncut stones. Spotted crystals, yellowish crystals or imperfectly formed crystals were relegated to the lower merchant and warrior classes and to other "inferior castes."

Rubies, which captured the intense redness of the visible spectrum and reflected back to the eye a brilliant color almost never seen in the otherwise rather brownish and dull-greenish surroundings where they were found, were also thought to be magical. The princes of Burma decreed five centuries ago that any ruby weighing over six carats should become the property of the royal household. On pain of death, miners had to surrender any large crystal.

Gems also partake of the mystery of color. Certain colors are central not only to philosophy but also to linguistic development in different cultures. An anthropological study by Brent Brolin and Paul Kay indicates that in any culture with only two words for color, white (all colors) and black (the absence of color) are the terms chosen. Where three words for color exist, white, black and red are selected. And where there are five words, red, blue, white, green (or yellow) and black are chosen. Thus, it is clear that the basic colors of red, blue and green are exceptionally important to various cultures throughout the world.

In England in the fourteenth century, every bishop, upon taking office, was presented with a sapphire ring. This ring, with its stone of a deep-blue color, symbolized the powers of heaven that were vested in the bishop—powers giving him both temporal and sacred rights to dispense blessings and judgments. On seeing the stirrup-shaped gem-set bishop's ring in the Victoria and Albert Museum, one is struck by the enormous effort that must have gone into its design and creation. The sapphire, a deep-blue Ceylon stone, had to be brought all the way from the East, through India, via the Middle East, across the sea and, finally, to England. At that time Ceylon was the principal source of fine-quality sapphires. Naturally, there is also the literary allusion in the biblical mention of sapphire-as the "Throne of God," in addition to references to sapphires in the heavenly city of Jerusalem. The sapphire ring was so important as an emblem of a medieval bishop's station in life that, after his death, his tomb would be surmounted by a life-size portrait sculpture in which, clearly visible to all, would be included a representation in stone of the stirrup-shaped sapphire ring.

Blue was sacred also to the Zuni and Navajo Indians of the American Southwest, in particular because of its relationship to the color of the sky. To them, however, it was turquoise which served as the visual echo of the enormous expanse of blue sky. Their religious and tribal leaders would all wear specially fine specimens of turquoise, for Navajo and Zuni legends speak of it as having been dropped from the heavens and of it being a sacred stone. Because of this, jewelry makers in these tribal cultures also enjoyed a high status and social position.

Gems partake of the mystery of the "faraway." Throughout the world people feel a fascination for what is distant and unknown. Tibet assumes an esoteric mystery in Western eyes because of its inaccessibility. Mount Everest, "because it is there," beckons to be visited, climbed and conquered. Forty-five hundred years ago, in what was then a center of civilization, the people of Ur wanted to honor Inanna, goddess of the morning and evening stars, and for this purpose only the rare blue lapis, shiny and lustrous, would do. The fact that lapis could be found only after an extensive and dangerous journey to snow-clad peaks thousands of miles away, in the forbidding mountains of present-day Afghanistan, made it most appropriate as a precious gift to Inanna. The sacred head-dress found in the tomb of Queen Pu-abi (and now on display in the British Museum), with its rows of extraordinarily blue lapis, becomes even more breathtaking when one considers the perils of the journey that had to be undertaken to procure the stones used by the Sumerian jeweller responsible for the creation of so regal an object.

Pearls brought to Europe from Bahrain, in the Persian Gulf, represented not just the fruits of a long voyage across the known world but also of the hidden recesses of the oceans. Joseph Hall, Bishop of Norwich (1574–1656), wrote:

> A fair pearl laid up in the bosom of the sea
> That was never seen nor never shall be.

The idea of a pearl as a shining and complete gift from the depths of the sea gave the wearer a traveler's souvenir "from far away."

Gems partake of the mystery of changeability. Hindu mystics regarded the world as an ever-changing river. Opals, because of the different levels of their molecular structure, reflect light in a magical, iridescent fashion. Depending upon the angle at which an opal is viewed, it will seem to change its personality. Its very fragility as a gemstone, and its susceptibility to changes in heat or humidity which can markedly alter its appearance, have given rise to the mystery of changeability that has contributed to the allure of opal. Sir Walter Scott has described the superstitious fear associated with opal arising from the very fact that its appearance is changeable. People may be drawn to or repelled by things that change, but change is always a source of mystery.

Gems also partake of the mystery of rarity. We are, all of us, searching for something unique. A type of demantoid garnet, found in one mountain range in Russia and in no other place in the world, held a particular fascination, by virtue of its rarity, for the nineteenth-century Russian aristocracy. In the same manner of thinking, a perfectly white and flawless diamond that can be tested with a microscope and "certified" by a gemological laboratory is extraordinarily rare and hence much sought after. A shimmering, vivid, naturally yellow diamond is even rarer and more sought after than its perfect white counterpart. How wonderful it must be to be able to wear a gem that is so rare that it is *hors concours*.

Gems have in the past been regarded as possessing therapeutic properties. In her book *Magical Jewels*, Joan Evans recounts how Jean de la Taille wrote in 1574 that diamond drives away "the terror that comes by night," emerald strengthens the memory and ruby brings joy. Dioscorides, a classical writer, informs us that lapis lazuli protects one against the bite of a serpent, and Pliny tells us that amber is a cure for goiter.

Stones have for centuries been regarded as emblematic of a person's hour and month of birth. Far from being merely a retail jeweler's vehicle for increasing sales, birthstones are a feature of many different cultures. In many societies gems are talismans of strength. To the Migration hordes that swept across Europe after the fall of Rome, garnets symbolized blood and hence virility and life. These fiery red stones were worn in battle in rings, belt-buckles, swords and brooches. A visitor to the British Museum, seeing the seventh-century excavated hoard, the Sutton Hoo treasure, realizes that not only did these warriors wear the garnet jewelry but that when they died they were also buried with it. The Lombards, the Avars, the Celts and the Visigoths all believed that garnets would give them power even in the hereafter.

Finally, and by no means least, precious stones have always been regarded as a source of "insurance value." The phrase "selling the family jewels" has always meant that precious stones are an "asset of the last resort"—to be disposed of only in times of runaway inflation, economic depression, revolution or personal crisis.

It is not surprising to note that in modern times, the stone that has come to be regarded as the middle-class symbol of personal wealth is the diamond. The reason for this is that, through the world supply being dominated by De Beers Consolidated Mines Ltd, the diamond has become the most "corporatized" of all gems. In gem qualities, however, at the top level of purity and perfection, a ruby and, on occasion, a gem emerald, are far more valuable, on a per-carat basis, because such stones are more than fifty times rarer than white diamonds of top quality.

In this book these mysteries of the allure of gems are discussed and probed fully, and an extensive discussion of the place gems occupy when set in jewelry is presented. The basic idea of a jewel is to enhance the innate properties and allure of a particular gem by providing an appropriate setting. In the Renaissance period, for example, Venetian jewelry designers were extraordinarily skilled in combining delicately colored enamels with rubies, sapphires and emeralds. In the early twentieth century the Art Nouveau jeweler René Lalique created a sumptuous ring containing a deep-color, rich Burma sapphire, in combination with a diaphanous *plique à jour* enamel setting. The quality of light passing through the sapphire contrasts markedly with the quality of light passing through the translucent enameled setting. Furthermore, enamel, by its nature, is fragile whereas sapphire is extremely hard and durable. This contradiction in aesthetic qualities appealed to Lalique and to the French Art Nouveau philosophy of aesthetics. The contradiction was seen as a mirror to the central conundrum of beauty: That which is most beautiful often seems to be short-lived.

In India the Mughal jewelers were able to thread tiny seed pearls in a delicate fashion and thereby highlight the beauty of diamonds, jade and other stones. The placement of the various gems in a ring in India has had an astrological significance, and the nine-stone ring set with different gems, the *naoratna*, has been and still is widely worn.

Oftentimes, the very shape of the gem will dictate the form of a piece of jewelry. The wondrous baroque pearl that suggests the body and shoulders of a man was set in the sixteenth century into the magnificent Canning Jewel (on display in the Victoria and Albert Museum). The fact that the jewel is in the form of Triton, the Greek god of the sea, makes all the more sense, as this pearl came from the waters off Bahrain.

In each chapter of this book there is an overall discussion of what shade of color for each gem is most preferable to the connoisseur. The different types of gem are seen, as it were, through the eyes of the gem dealer. In each case they arc traced from the mine source, through the gem merchant's hands and into the hands of the designer and jewelry manufacturer. Superb examples of jewels containing gems are illustrated, with the idea that the reader can visualize what a master craftsman can create with gem material. Also, information on how gems can be tested and differentiated from synthetics and imitations is offered.

Finally, the book includes a guide to public collections where important and beautiful gems can be seen, as well as a discussion of some outstanding jewels in private ownership.

ONE

RUBY

"When a ruby exceeds six carats and is perfect,
it is sold for whatever is asked for it."

The Six Voyages of Jean-Baptiste Tavernier (1676)

ERFECTION, TO THE French explorer Jean-Baptiste Tavernier (1605-89), was to be found in a beautiful, full-bodied red ruby, the kind of gem that he could bring home from India for his royal client, Louis XIV, and persuade the king to pay for in gold. Tavernier was a gem merchant who made six voyages to India, each of at least three years' duration. On the way he stopped in Constantinople (now Istanbul), Samarkand, Kabul, Delhi, Jaipur, Golconda and in Ceylon (Sri Lanka). Toward the end of his life, Tavernier wrote an account of the Mughal and Deccan courts and the trade in precious stones there. He described the bargaining that could often stretch over a period of months and the canniness of the Indian gem-sellers. More importantly, he accurately described and drew the outstanding examples of rubies and diamonds that he saw.

How did Tavernier, and how do we, judge whether a ruby is a gemstone? Scientifically, both ruby and sapphire have the same structural composition, corundum. They are composed of aluminum oxide (Al_2O_3), but the presence of tiny traces of chromium oxide makes corundum red, and the resultant crystalline material is called "ruby." All other shades of corundum—blue, yellow, green, purple, pink and orange—are termed sapphire (*see* chapter 2). Rubies (with their requisite traces of chromium) are exceedingly rare and have always been valued at three or more times the price of sapphires. Natural deposits of chromium, unlike aluminum oxide, occur in only a few places on earth. It is not surprising, therefore, that the combination of aluminum oxide and chromium occurs so rarely.

Although rubies are characterized by a single color, red, they occur in many different shades—red is never simply red. The rubies which Tavernier was seeking were of the same type as those which ruby connoisseurs still search for today—stones of a deep, rich red color without any overlay of an orange, pink, purple or, still worse, a brownish cast. The finest red is called "pigeon blood," this being a term used by Indian gem dealers over the past two millennia to describe the shade occurring in the centre of the red spectrum. Unmistakably vivid in its purity, "pigeon blood" is, in the oriental definition, quoted by the eminent Swiss gemologist, Dr Eduard Gübelin: "The hue of the first two drops of blood which appear in the nostrils of a freshly shot pigeon." In the West the intense red shade of the hybrid rose Happiness corresponds to the pigeon-blood red of gem rubies. Less than one in twenty-thousand rubies would have this pure red shade. Burma rubies occasionally have the right combination of aluminum, oxygen and traces of chromium that produces this vivid red color.

It may take many years of comparing shades of red to develop a connoisseurship in rubies. The essential method used by a gem merchant is to lay one ruby alongside others. By constantly comparing the rubies, one's eye adapts to the different nuances of the shades of red. Of course, this connoisseurship is difficult to attain. Normally, one heeds expert advice when deciding on a substantial purchase of rubies. Traditionally, the very fine jewelry stores have provided such guidance.

The shades of red, as gem dealers know, will vary markedly, depending on the light source used. A ruby viewed in India, with its brilliant sunlight and clear skies, appears to be much brighter and purer than does the same stone studied in an overcast northern European climate. It is perhaps for this reason that rubies have always been treasured far more in the East than in Europe or America.

In Ceylon rubies there are fewer traces of chromium and the stones tend to have a pinkish cast. This pink shade gives a softer, more watery look. Placed alongside a fine pigeon-blood ruby, the Ceylon stone tends to lose its clarity and for this reason is not as highly prized or as greatly sought after by connoisseurs.

Rubies mined in Thailand are red but contain more traces of iron. This gives the stones a purplish and often a brownish cast, resulting in a more muddy red. In the "pecking order" of rubies, the Thai ruby is considered less desirable than the Ceylon or Burma. However, extremely high prices are now being paid for Thai rubies if they are of a pure color and are lively.

Finally, there is a newcomer, the African ruby, which often is even darker and more brownish in tone than the Thai.

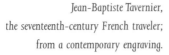

*Jean-Baptiste Tavernier,
the seventeenth-century French traveler;
from a contemporary engraving.*

Historically, because of the lack of suitable instruments (microscope, spectroscope) to aid identification, red rubies were often confused with other red stones, such as garnet and spinel. Indeed, spinel frequently was termed "balas ruby," the word "balas" probably coming from Balascia, ancient capital of the province of Badakhshan, in Afghanistan.

Tavernier tells a tale of Shah Jahan and his son, Aurangzeb, who imprisoned his father (who built the Taj Mahal) and then had the effrontery to take him a stone and ask him if it was a ruby of incredible value or a balas ruby. From his cell across the river from the Taj Mahal, Shah Jahan pronounced the stone to be a balas ruby and not worth the 95,000 rupees (1,425,000 livres) that Aurangzeb had paid for it. The great Mughal quite promptly insisted that the gem dealer who sold him the stone take it back, but he still left his father imprisoned.

Ruby mines in Burma go back to prehistoric times. At the mining site at Mogok, in the upper reaches of Burma, Stone Age tools have been found, indicating the antiquity of the site. Over the centuries, if any ruby weighing over six carats was found, it became the property of the ruler of Burma. The miners had to depend upon the munificence of successive rulers to repay them adequately for a stone of large size and extraordinary beauty. Consequently, many large pieces of rough stones were immediately split up into smaller, non-taxable, six-carat sizes or less.

From 1888 to 1931 the Burma mines were run by a British company, Burma Ruby Mines Ltd, employing relatively modern dredging equipment. By using flooding techniques and water jets, miners removed large quantities of over-burden and extracted precious ruby crystals, both from river beds and river banks. By the end of the 1980s, however, the mines were relatively exhausted and virtually no important new Burmese rubies were found. Thus, after five thousand years of mining, the supply had nearly dried up, but what do still exist today are gem rubies mined many years ago, among them stones in princely collections in India, gems in the fine retail stores and in the inventories of deal-ers, and—scattered throughout the world—privately owned, treasured family heirlooms, rubies worn in rings, brooches or necklaces.

In the middle 1990s, in the Mong Hsu area in north-eastern Myanmar (Burma), new Burma ruby veins were located and mined. To the connoisseur, these stones generally do not have the pure, seductive, intense red color of the old-time "pigeon-blood" ruby. For a while, the Mong Hsu ruby was sold to undiscerning buyers as Burma ruby. The American Gemological Laboratory, headed by C. R. "Cap" Beesley has established and trademarked the term "clas-sic" (Mogok) to distinguish the highly desirable old-mine variety of ruby from the more pinkish, less saturated new Burmese production.

Rubies in Vietnam have also been discovered, mined, and merchandised throughout the world. While they are more pinkish than their aristocratic, deep-red Burmese relations, they have filled a definite need because of the terrific drop in the supply of classic Burmese rubies.

The Ceylon ruby diggings have been mined as far back, at least, as the sec-ond century. Marco Polo (1254–1324), in the course of his travels, describes seeing the mines. The mining methods employed today in Sri Lanka (Ceylon) are strikingly similar to those used in Marco Polo's day. The mysterious original source of rubies somewhere in the mountains of central Ceylon has never been found. Water takes corundum (ruby and sapphire) rough and scatters it, via rivers, throughout the island. Using a method much like that of the prospector panning for gold, Sri Lanka miners, with baskets and panning equipment, recover and sift the gem-bearing gravel painstakingly by hand.

Along with corundum, a treasure chest of other gem material is found—

1 *A 5.88-carat Burma ruby of pigeon-blood color, set in a pavé diamond ring. The term "pigeon blood,"
used in Sanskrit manuscripts to describe the color of the blood that appears in the nostrils of a freshly
killed pigeon, is a connoisseur's phrase for the most desirable and the purest shade of red in rubies.*

2 *A gem-quality brilliant 2.86-carat Thai ruby with a typically Burma color. Occasionally, Thai rubies will have the rich, saturated classical Burma Color.*

3 *A brilliant Thai ruby. While the red of this ruby has too much brown for it to be termed a pigeon-blood color, the stone possesses an unusual brilliance and depth of color which make it a true gem. Thai rubies are accepted today and sought after if they are relatively free from inclusions and are of a high color.*

4 *A gem pink Ceylon oval ruby, 2.58 carats. This ruby has jun, the Persian connoisseur's term for "life." The dividing line between ruby and sapphire is one of degree. If this stone had slightly more blue in it, it would be termed a pink sapphire.*

5 (BELOW) *A range of color in a group of rubies.* LEFT, *pinkish-red stones mined in Ceylon;* CENTER, *brownish-red stones from Thailand;* SECOND FROM RIGHT, *a deep, richly colored ruby from Burma.*

6 (ABOVE) Rubies in a calcite crystal; only rarely are rubies found in situ, as this one was. Generally, they are water-worn crystals with rounded edges. Occasionally, such ruby rough is found in Burma, but is not cut because of its beauty as a crystal specimen.

7 A star ruby. In such stones the "star" results from the presence of crossed rutile needles. The cutter must orient the crystal rough so as to have the star appear on the very top of the cabochon. When seen in brilliant sunshine, as in the Far East, the appearance of the stone is magnificent.

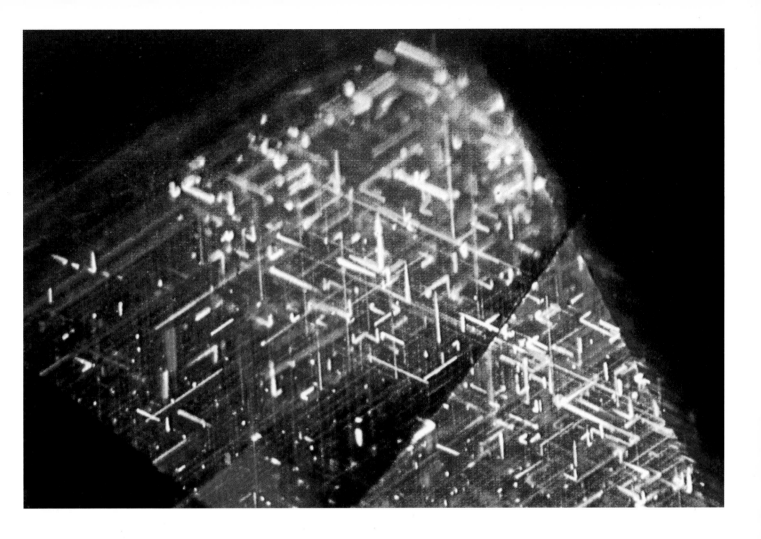

8 (ABOVE) Rutile needles interwoven in a Burma ruby. When viewed under a microscope, the dense character indicates both the origin of the stone and provides proof of its genuineness.

9 An Art Deco ring, c. 1925 set with the finest shade of Burma rubies. The art of the jeweler is to surround the center stone with rubies in a way to give color to the ring.

10 Most rubies occur in melee sizes of one-tenth of a carat. The dark purple stones in the upper portion are those with the least desirable color. The stones in each parcel of melee have to be graded and separated into different shades of red. Rubies of these two- and three-millimeter sizes are used commercially.

11 (BELOW) Ruby melee much magnified. Even two-millimeter round rubies such as these can be hand-cut by young cutters in Thailand to give at least twenty facets. After an apprenticeship of several years during which they work only on small stones, cutters graduate to stones of over one carat.

12 *A beautiful matched suite of one-carat Burma rubies. Bracelets of color-matched rubies are exceptionally rare today. Here, eighteen stones were recut so as to be matched in size, brilliance, symmetry and color.*

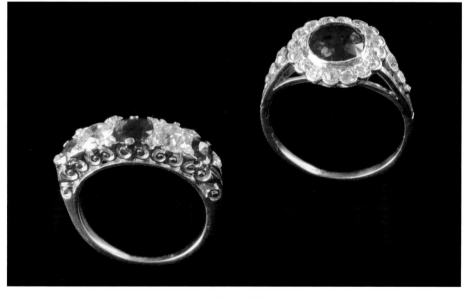

13 *Two 19th century rings showing the purest shade of the classic Burma ruby color.*

14 Ruby mining in Sri Lanka. Rubies are mined today in essentially the same way as in Marco Polo's day. Miners sift alluvial material using baskets (the same technique as used when panning for gold); the mud falls through, leaving any ruby crystals in the basket.

15 Once panned, the crystals are first sorted and separated by shape. Subsequently, the ruby crystals are sold to Colombo gem cutters who then cut and polish them.

16 (ABOVE) *Rubies are mined in Chanthaburi, Thailand. No heavy equipment is used in mining lest the fragile ruby crystals be damaged. Typically, a miner may work for at least one month before finding a piece of rough ruby crystal weighing over one carat.*

17 *A miner in Chanthaburi. Mining is primarily a family affair, with the father going down into a pit ten or fifteen feet deep with primitive scraping equipment, and the mother and children hoisting up the stones he collects by means of pulleys.*

18 (ABOVE) *A nineteenth-century cabochon ruby and emerald bracelet made in Jaipur (cf. ill. 80).*

19 *Diamond, ruby, and natural pearl Dutch earrings, c. 1680. The diamonds mined in India were cut into "rose" cuts in Amsterdam.*

20 Necklace and earrings, consisting of cabochon rubies and diamonds, by Cartier of Paris.

21, 22 (BELOW) *A gimmel ring. In Renaissance times a ruby had the religious connotation of charity, with the emerald symbolizing faith. This south German ring, dated 1631, comes apart to form two separate rings. On the inside of the shank are two "memento mori" figures, reminding the wearer of the transience of life, the baby representing life, and the skeleton, death.*

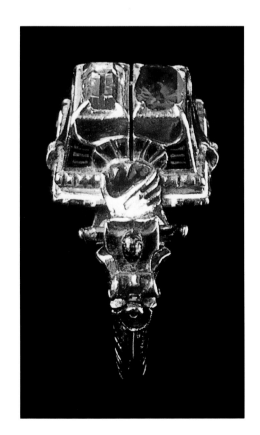

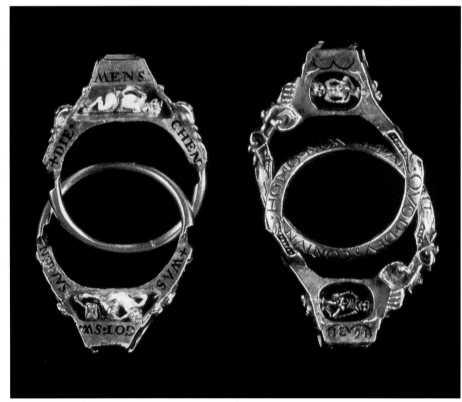

23 The Imperial State Crown in the British Crown Jewels, remade for the coronation of Queen Victoria in 1838. The pearl-bordered circlet is set with gemstones, including the 317.40-carat diamond known as the Second Star of Africa (Cullinan II), above which is the so-called Black Prince's Ruby. This large polished stone, formerly thought to be a ruby, is in fact a spinel (or "balas ruby") with a history going back to the fourteenth century.

spinel, garnet, chrysoberyl. Red garnet and red spinel are distinguished from the ruby crystals, not by their color but by the shape of the crystal. Ruby always crystallizes in the same six-sided prism (hexagonal form), terminated by flat faces. Even though a ruby's crystal faces are often water worn, they are distinct from the octahedral (diamond or lozenge shape) spinel crystals.

In Thailand (Siam) commercial ruby mining started in the 1930s. There, a rudimentary pit is often dug by hand. The use of blasting equipment to remove the overburden would shatter the delicate ruby crystals, and for this reason no such methods are used. The major Thai mines are in Chanthaburi or across the border in Cambodia, in Phailin, fifty miles east of Battam bang. Both areas are extremely unsafe today because of guerrilla activity and political instability. In addition, like the Sri Lankan and Burmese mines, Thai sources are showing signs of exhaustion.

In mining, the old days are the good days. It is a peculiar geological phenomenon that the rubies nearest the surface of the earth are the largest and their color is the strongest and purest. As one starts digging deeper into the ground, the crystals diminish in size and the color becomes less pure and less saturated. This phenomenon occurs, perhaps, because of the increased pressure at greater depth. In any case, as the mine continues to be used, the crystal structure is broken down, both in size and color strength. Within the Sri Lankan and Thai ruby mines, the same phenomenon has long been observed and understood by gem connoisseurs. Because gem rubies have become scarcer, and because demand has become more widespread, prices have increased geometrically. Naturally, only a completely new mine would provide a major new source of gem-quality rubies.

In the early 1960s a promising source was discovered in Kenya. Because of the exhaustion of the other mining areas, it was hoped that this new source of supply might be able to satisfy the world's increasing thirst for fine rubies. The quality of the Kenya stones, however, turned out to be not as fine as the Burmese. The color was often too muddy and the material itself not as transparent and brilliant as rubies from Thailand and Sri Lanka. Similarly, a new ruby deposit has been found near Fiskenaesset in southwestern Greenland; in spite of extensive exploration, however, no important quantity of gem-quality stones has resulted.

Once the crystal is recovered from the ground, the rough ruby has to be cut, faceted (i.e. flat surfaces are ground on the stone) and polished. In the case of a ruby crystal of two carats or more, the procedure can take a long time. It is not that the cutting process takes long, but rather that there are so many planning decisions to be made. The angles at which the stone is cut, the size of the ultimate stone and the arrangement of the facets are of paramount importance. Rubies are pleochroic, that is, they have both red and purple in them. Depending on the angle of cutting relative to the optic axis, the cut stone will appear to be either red or purple. The cutter will try to cut the stone so as to have the purest red showing through the top, or table, of the stone. The skill in cutting lies in wresting the largest, most pure gemstone from the piece of rough. Often, the question will be posed as to whether the cutter should try for a large, impure stone, or for a smaller stone, free of internal inclusions (microscopic liquid or solid matter). Increasingly today, the preference is for a smaller stone with fewer imperfections.

The piece of ruby rough is fixed with an adhesive to a wooden dop stick and pressed against a diamond-impregnated copper lap (wheel). Flat facets are thus fashioned against a turning wheel. The facets are exceedingly important, as even a slight change in the angles will alter the path that light takes within the stone. If the ruby's proportions are not correct, the stone will be rather "dead" in appearance. A stone that has a lot of brilliance is termed one that has "life." Even more important than life to a ruby, however, is its basic color. Any connoisseur will prefer a deep-red ruby with an unsightly inclusion in the center to a brownish-red, perfectly flawless stone. Interestingly, in the West, proportion and balance in cutting are highly valued, but in the East, color is more appreciated and symmetry is not so highly prized.

Cutting styles since the eighteenth century have not changed all that much. The arrangement of facets on a twentieth-century ruby is quite similar to that of a fifteenth-century stone. Before the fifteenth century, gemstones were cut in a cabochon form—that is, with a rounded top and no flat facets. After the discovery of the principles of faceting, gem-cutters were thereby able to impart greater brilliance to a stone by smoothing its edges. With the advent of faceting, the internal world of ruby became more noticeable.

Inside each ruby, often visible to the naked eye and most certainly when viewed through a microscope, is a diary of the stone's crystallization. While the ruby crystal was developing in the ground, foreign matter such as liquid, spinel crystals, mica crystals and zircon crystals may have been trapped within it. These inclusions, which neophytes term "flaws," tell us a great deal about where a particular stone comes from, under what geological conditions it was formed and if, indeed, it is a genuine or synthetic stone.

In Burma stones there is often a peculiar interlocking web of rutile needles. These needles intersect one another at 60° angles and are woven densely together, giving an appearance of "silk" under the microscope. According to Dr. Gübelin, in his landmark study, *The Internal World of Gemstones*, the rutile in Burma stones tends to be of a different nature from the rutile present in Ceylon rubies. In the latter it is more slender and less finely woven. (If a ruby cabochon can be cut so that these criss-cross rutile needles reflect in a star-like pattern, the result is called a "star ruby"; the "star" is seen when light from an outside, non-fluorescent, source is shone directly on the stone.) In a Thai ruby or an African ruby, there is no silk at all. Detecting such interlocking rutile under 10X – 40X (ten- to forty-power) magnification gives one a clue to the origin of the stone. On a magnificent tenth-century bejeweled book cover in the Pierpont Morgan Library, New York, one may see corundum with slender rutile needles—proof that the stones came from Ceylon. Obviously, to set Thai rubies in such a book cover, dating from the tenth century, would have been impossible, or their presence would indicate that the stones had been added later. After the eighteenth century, many large cabochon rubies were removed from crowns, book covers and historic pieces of jewelry and re-cut into a faceted form. In addition, stones often were taken from mountings and substituted with either glass or stones of poorer quality. A careful study of inclusions can often be of considerable help in determining when a historic piece of jewelry was fashioned.

Solid inclusions within rubies are exceedingly beautiful when viewed under a microscope. One might see, for example, a zircon crystal trapped within a Ceylon ruby. The Ceylon stones are, gemologically speaking, of more recent date than those of Burma. Burma rubies often contain zircon crystals without a halo surrounding them. Ceylon zircon inclusions, on the other hand, do have a halo around them.

The interior world of gemstones is a panoply of lakes of liquid, mountains of crystals and mineral "flora" and "fauna." One needs only a microscope to examine them. The concept of flawlessness, so important in a diamond, is not of very much commercial or aesthetic importance in a ruby. A characteristic feature of inclusions in ruby, and indeed in all gemstones, is that shapes are formed naturally in straight lines and flat planes. By contrast, one sees curved lines and rounded gas bubbles in synthetic stones. If, when examining a ruby under the microscope, one sees a curved line, this is certain proof that the stone is synthetic.

There are other methods to distinguish between natural and synthetic ruby. Under longwave and shortwave ultraviolet light, synthetic stones tend to fluoresce very, very strongly—in a bright-red color. The fluorescence of Burma ruby is less bright, while that of a Ceylon ruby is a brilliant red. The iron component that gives Thai rubies their brownish and purplish cast also serves to deaden their fluorescence. A spectroscope can be used to further separate synthetic from genuine stones. Similarly, one can separate a ruby scientifically from its natural gemstone counterparts—garnet and spinel—by testing it on a refractometer. This instrument measures the "bending" of light within a stone. Rubies, garnets and spinels each have different refractive indices, as they bend light to a different degree, and can thus be distinguished one from another.

In recent years, virtually every newly mined ruby containing rutile inclusions has been submitted to various degrees of "heat enhancement." Generally, the treatment occurs when the ruby is in its rough "uncut" state. What this heating does is to melt the rutile needles and vastly improve the color. The improvement is considered permanent. However, to a connoisseur, the fact that this has been an altered state makes the stone less valuable and desirable.

Generally speaking, each ruby of significant value is accompanied by a laboratory certificate stating that the stone is either heat-enhanced or free from heat enhancement. (See documentary illustrations, pp. 288 and 239)

Fine rubies are becoming exceedingly rare. Aside from perhaps visiting one's grandmother and seeing the ruby ring she wears, one can view items for sale at leading auction houses, or visit fine retail stores and museum collections to observe the fabulous shades of red occurring in the finest specimens. In the Sorbonne in Paris, one can see a ruby rough crystal still embedded in white calcite. The redness of that ruby is pigeon blood, and its contrast to the white calcite makes it all the more dramatic. The De Long star ruby in the American Museum of Natural History, New York, and the Rosser Reeves star ruby in the Smithsonian Institution in Washington offer examples of the clarity and depth of color of a star stone. In the Residenz Palace in Munich, there is a stunning figure of St. George mounted on a horse; the color of the rubies that stud the equestrian gear is of a pigeon-blood hue. Perhaps the finest single ruby jewel in the world is a belt-buckle now in the Iranian Bank Melli, Tehran. The buckle contains twenty finely matched, incredibly pure-red, Burma ruby cabochons, and many of these individual stones weigh over ten carats.

Obviously, values for rubies are difficult to quote because they depend upon the purity of color, the perfection of crystallization and the size of the stone. The collection of gems in the Iranian Bank Melli are together worth over $5 billion today, and serve as a backing for the national currency of Iran.

The Hindus called ruby *ratna raj*, the king of precious stones. John Ruskin called it "the loveliest precious stone of which I have any knowledge." In both the East and the West, connoisseurs would all agree that ruby, when it is of gem quality, is one of the great glories of nature.

T W O
SAPPHIRE

"When God resolved to bring a flood upon the earth, He sent the archangel Raphael to Noah, bearing the message, "I give you a holy book with all the secrets and mysteries of the universe." Noah took the book and studied it. The book was made of sapphire. All the time Noah spent in the ark, it served him as a timepiece, to distinguish night from day. Before his death, he entrusted it to Shem and he in turn to Abraham. From Abraham the sapphire descended through Jacob to Levi and then to Moses, Joshua and Solomon. Solomon learned all his wisdom from it, his skill in the healing art, and his mastery over the demons."

—LOUIS GINZBERG, *Legends of the Bible*

SAPPHIRE, WITH ITS magnificent blue color, has always been central to the human spiritual and aesthetic sense. Marco Polo journeyed from Constantinople through Samarkand, across the Gobi Desert into Cathay, with sapphires as his calling cards. The stones he presented to the Khan, as well as his charm as a storyteller, earned him the post of merchant-ambassador in the court of the Khan.

Ceylon (Sri Lanka)—the country that was Marco Polo's chief source of sapphires (and rubies) some centuries ago—continues to be the principal source of sapphires today, although the supply is not as plentiful as before. A few sapphires have survived from Marco Polo's day. Some are embedded in bejeweled book covers, and a very few have survived either set in rings or in loose form. Until the fifteenth century, it was almost impossible to facet a sapphire. Consequently, sapphires were cut by hand in cabochon form, in the same manner as rubies.

One example of an English bishop's ring of the thirteenth century incorporates a sapphire from Marco Polo's day. Perhaps it is one of the stones that Marco Polo himself brought back and scattered before the incredulous Venetian doge to prove that his stories were indeed true.

An interesting sapphire in the form of a semi-faceted cabochon was uncovered

at the archaeological site of Polonnaruwa, the thirteenth-century Buddhist center in
Ceylon. In addition to having an amuletic animal shape, this stone catches the light
because of its ridges and is the earliest known example of a semi-faceted cabochon.
Interestingly enough, the treatment of this sapphire matches that of another stone,
the second one being in the Harari Collection (S. J Phillips, London). That stone is
said to have been set in Alexandria, a way station between Ceylon and Europe for
the traffic in gems.

*Marco Polo
(1254–1324) and
Kublai Khan, at
whose court the
famous Venetian
traveler was first
received in 1275.*

What were the qualities that Marco Polo and other early gem dealers were looking for in sapphires? Basically, they were the same ones for which their merchant
counterparts search today, primarily the purity of the blue color. Like ruby, sapphire
is aluminum oxide (Al_2O_3), corundum. The presence of tiny additional traces of
titanium oxide and iron oxide creates the blue color. If oxides of chromium, titanium and iron are present together, a purple sapphire is the result. A yellow sapphire
is created with iron oxide alone as an admixture to aluminum oxide. Ruby (red
corundum) comes about, as we have noted, when traces of chromium oxide combine with aluminum oxide. Although sapphire also occurs in yellow, orange, purple and green, it is the blue shade that historically has been most sought after.
Marco Polo was searching for the pure, perfect and platonic blue, a blue without
any admixture of gray, green, violet or black. The majority of sapphires coming
from Ceylon, however, have been characterized by an overtone of gray.

Most of the historical sapphires in the so-called crown of Charlemagne, for
example, or in the magnificent medieval book covers in the Pierpont Morgan
Library, are pronouncedly gray. One such cover—itself clearly the artistic apogee of
the Northern European Romanesque world—contains the most delicate gold and

silver work combined with sapphires of only indifferent quality embedded in prong settings. One must remember, however, that in the early Middle Ages, this type of grey-blue sapphire was the best quality available in the Western world. To the Mosan jeweler, and indeed to the medieval mind, the very color of blue was important, even though the shade was not a pure rich blue. The color blue was emblematic of heaven and was treasured for that reason.

For purity of blue in sapphire, the Burma mines were a godsend. There, a deep shade of blue, a royal blue, was occasionally present in a stone, and Burma sapphires became sought after by gem connoisseurs. Typically, a connoisseur will take a Burma stone and lay it alongside other sapphires to compare nuances of the shade of blue. More important than the size of the stone is the question of secondary colors. The Ceylon blue at its finest has a cornflower cast to it. This is a lighter shade of blue, but exceedingly lively, whereas the richer color of Burma stones of the finest quality tends more to a royal blue.

After the faceting of stones was improved in the fifteenth and sixteenth centuries, Ceylon stones were appreciated even more. The inherent brilliance and life of a Ceylon sapphire was all the more impressive when flat edges were placed on the crystal rough. What the Ceylon stone lacked in color, it more than made up for in fire.

These two sources, however, still do not produce the finest-quality sapphire. Pride of place in the sapphire mining areas of the world is given to a remote corner of the northwestern Himalayas—Kashmir. According to David Atkinson and Rustan Z. Kothvala, in an article "Kashmir Sapphires" (*Gems and Gemology*, Summer 1983), in 1881 a rock slide on the high slopes of the Zanskar range of mountains exposed sapphire-bearing rock. For about fifty years, some extraordinary gems were mined there. The blue of the Kashmir sapphire became proverbial, an intense rich shade which did not change in sunlight or artificial light (unlike a Burma or a Ceylon stone that tended to lose color—what gem dealers call "bleed color"—slightly in artificial light).

The color of Kashmir sapphires was so exceptional that the description "Kashmir" was also applied to Ceylon or Burma stones if they happened to have this top shade of blue. Kashmir sapphires are also somewhat sleepy in appearance because of internal inclusions. This characteristic notwithstanding, however, the Kashmir shade often makes other sapphire blues appear greenish or grayish when the stones are viewed side by side. Gem connoisseurs in India say that this pure blue Kashmir color resembles the hue of the peacock's neck feathers.

In the 1930s a new source of sapphire was discovered outside Bangkok, in Thailand. While often having very good luster, these stones, after cutting, tend to be blackish or greenish blue. Large quantities of sapphires in the rough form are coming from Queensland, Australia, and being sent to gem cutters in Bangkok, where they are mixed in with the Thai material. Because both the Kashmir and the Burma sapphire mines are virtually exhausted, gem connoisseurs have been hoping that new sources will become available. New mines have been opening in Cambodia as well as in Africa. However, the shades of color of stones from these sources—the Cambodian being somewhat inky and the African a bit watery—have not altered the overall "pecking order" of sapphire mines. The top quality remains Kashmir, the second, Burma and the third, Ceylon.

Muslim cutters remain in Sri Lanka (Ceylon) as part of a centuries-old tradition of faceting sapphires. Faceting secrets have been passed from father to son through the generations since Muslims first came to Ceylon in the tenth century. Unlike diamond, where the color is spread uniformly throughout the crystal, sapphire rough poses a great intellectual challenge to the cutter. Color often appears in greater concentrations in one part of the crystal than in other parts. The Ceylonese cutter also must cope with the fact that in all sapphires there are two dichroic shades of color—blue and violet—depending upon the direction of the optic axis of the crystal rough. The cutter must orient the stone so that, after cutting, the blue color is reflected through the table (top) of the stone. Typically, a sapphire looked at through the side, or girdle, will appear slightly violet or purplish violet. In addition to orienting the stone correctly, the cutter must see to it that the section of rough bearing the most intense color be faceted so that this color is reflected through the table, upwards toward the eye of the viewer.

Whereas in the West modern industrial processes have given rise to the idea that "time is money," the concept of time is different in the East. Production-line technology does not work in sapphire, and discussions among cutters in Sri Lanka can last many months before a stone is finished. All phases of sapphire mining and cutting are regarded with religious significance. Before a mine is opened, the (generally) Buddhist miners will consult an astrologer and religious figure for a propitious date and hour to begin the search for sapphire. Frequent offerings will be made during the mining period. Once the precious crystals have been wrested from the ground, they will be passed on to a cutter and a merchant who has "a good hand." Such a merchant is typically a traditional dealer who, it is said, if he touches the stone with his hand, will bring it good luck.

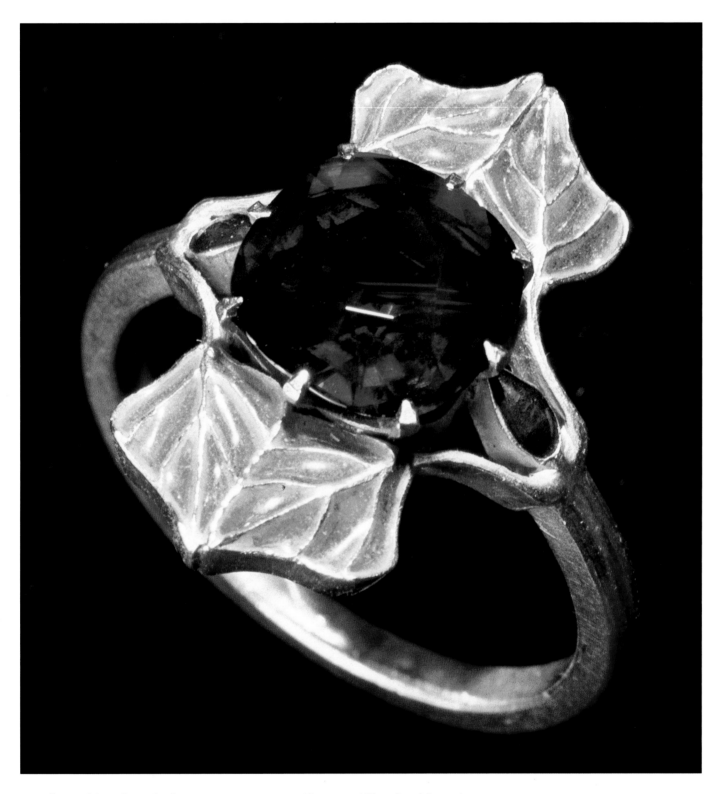

24 *A fine sapphire set by René Lalique in an Art Nouveau ring. The saturated blue color of the sapphire contrasts markedly with the diaphanous effect of the surrounding* plique à jour *enamel design characteristic of the Art Nouveau style at the turn of the century.*

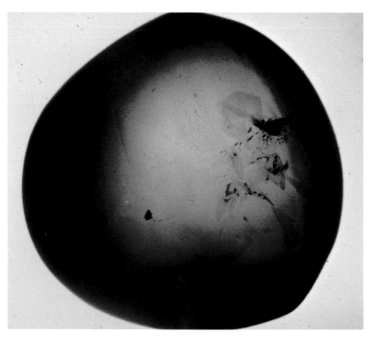

25, 26 (ABOVE) *A Burma star sapphire, weighing 94 carats. This stone was on loan to the American Museum of Natural History and displayed next to the Star of India, the Midnight Star and the De Long Star Ruby. Its color was considered to be the finest of any star sapphires on public display. When viewed under magnification, the same sapphire reveals a black dot—a zircon inclusion —in the upper portion of the stone, which does not have a radioactive halo around it (thus indicating a Burmese origin). Inclusions, rather than the shade of color, are the most reliable guide to a sapphire's origin.*

27 (ABOVE) *Two gem Kashmir sapphires (4.09 and 4.36 carats respectively). They contain no trace of gray, green or violet, and are of a specimen color. The unique Kashmir shade of blue is maintained both in sunlight and in incandescent and fluorescent light. Burma sapphires, as well as those from Ceylon, often appear to lose some of their color under certain conditions.*

28 *The interior of a Kashmir sapphire. A stone will often contain thin straight lines having a cloudy edge to them. This phenomenon is caused by the colloidal suspension of color within the crystal. Kashmir sapphires also reveal a characteristic velvety, hazy quality.*

29 *A fine gem-quality royal-blue Burma sapphire. The choicest Burma stones display a shade of blue that is rich and deep.*

30 *A liquid "feather" inside a Burma stone. This "feather," a scalloped edge, has been likened by Dr. Eduard Gübelin, the eminent Swiss gemologist, to a crumpled flag, and is a characteristic feature of sapphires from Burma. If the feather has a rounded edge, the stone can be identified as having originated in Ceylon.*

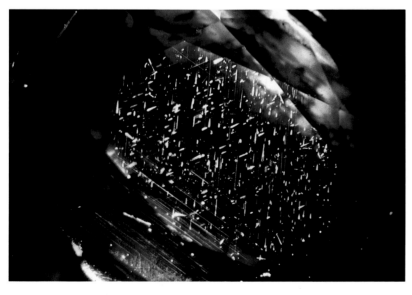

31 *A silk inclusion; this effect is created by a dense, criss-cross pattern of rutile needles that crystallized along with the host sapphire while it was "growing." The nature of the silk is evidence that the stone came from Burma (cf. ill. 33).*

32 *A fine Ceylon sapphire with a hint of gray. Gray is often characteristic of sapphires mined in Ceylon, which display a great deal of liveliness and "fire."*

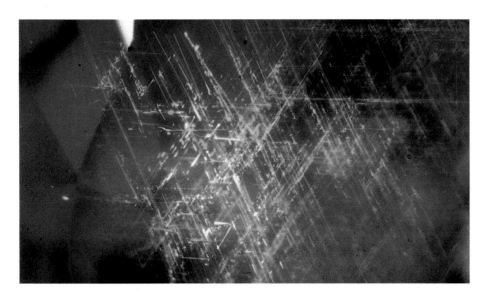

33 The interior of a Ceylon sapphire, greatly magnified. Here, rutile needles form a loosely woven silk, and are a sign that the stone came from Ceylon (cf. ill. 31).

34 *A zircon inclusion embedded in a Ceylon sapphire; the meteor-like appearance is the result of a radioactive halo around the zircon.*

35 *An Art Nouveau ring in a flower basket design, French, c. 1910, with the vivid sapphire blue and white diamond heads.*

36 (BELOW) *The range of colors occurring in sapphires.* LEFT, *a royal-blue Burma stone;* CENTER, *an intense Kashmir stone;* RIGHT, *pale, grayish-blue stones from Ceylon.*

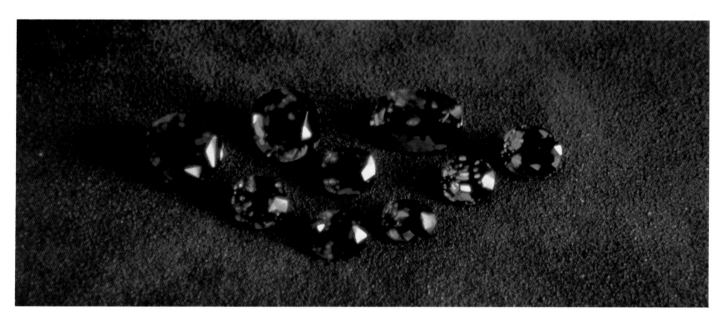

37 *An Art Deco ring, c. 1925 set with "skyscraper" like thin diamond baguettes highlighted by intensely blue sapphires.*

38 (ABOVE, LEFT) A bishop's ring from the late thirteenth century. This type of stirrup-shaped ring was presented to English bishops and worn as a symbol of office. Because of the depth of its blue color, the sapphire was believed to convey the blessings of heaven. Examples of such rings are in the Victoria and Albert Museum and the British Museum.

39 (ABOVE, RIGHT) A magnificent carved sapphire cameo. Sapphire was rarely used in the Greek and Roman periods. Technically, sapphire is much more difficult to engrave, because of its hardness, than garnet or semi-precious stones. Also, the great rarity of the sapphire made it exceedingly expensive.

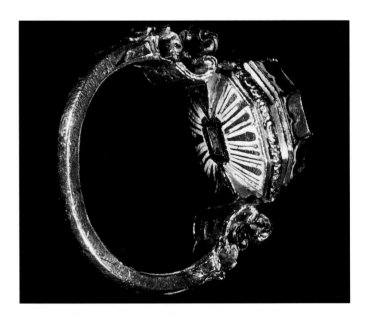

40, 41 A magnificent Renaissance sapphire ring. In sixteenth-century Italy, sapphires were foiled on the underside to give them extra brilliance. The combination of the blue of the stone plus the delicacy of the enameling make this ring a magnificent sculptured object, every portion of a ring being lavishly detailed, as can be seen in a view of the bottom of the bezel. Today, simpler prong settings emphasizing the stone are more in vogue.

42 (LEFT) *A gold ring set with a sapphire. The sapphire was probably set in the Greek colony of Alexandria in the fifth century* BC. *This unique ring provides evidence that semi-faceted cabochons were exported from Ceylon, via the Middle East, to Europe.*

43 (ABOVE) *An Art Nouveau sapphire, emerald, and diamond ring, French, c. 1910. The beautifully matched sapphires, carefully cut to fit the mounting, as well as the emeralds, present a colorful scrolling surround to the round diamond.*

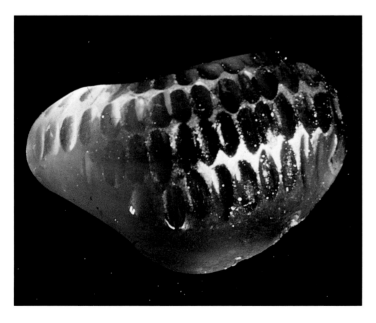

44 Kashmir sapphire ring. This 10.5-carat stone is set in platinum, and combined with trilliant-cut diamonds.

45 A Ceylon sapphire showing a change in cutting style. This is both a cabochon and a rudimentarily faceted stone; excavated at a thirteenth-century site, it represents the transition from the use of cabochons to the cutting of multifaceted gems.

46 (ABOVE, LEFT) *A fourteenth-century Ceylon green sapphire ring (a zircon inclusion shows that the stone is from Ceylon). This pie-dish bezeled ring dating from the time of Marco Polo gives evidence of Ceylonese stones having been exported all the way to England in the fourteenth century.*

47 (ABOVE, RIGHT) *A medieval ring (fifteenth-century) containing a sapphire. This ring is from the collection of Joan Evans, the well-known author of books on the history of jeweler.*

48 The Founder's Jewel. *A medieval letter jewel, "M," for Mary, in Lombardic script, was bequeathed to New College, Oxford, in 1404 by the college's founder, William of Wykeham. Here, a nineteenth-century reproduction of the jewel by Alessandro Castellani is shown; in order to give a feeling of antiquity, the jeweler incorporated two tenth-century sapphires formerly used in sapphire-bead necklaces.*

49 *A twentieth-century pendant consisting of a portrait cameo, artfully carved in Roman times, set in a Renaissance frame; from the frame is suspended an eleventh-century polished sapphire bead, in which the long, hollow, whitish space can be seen running lengthwise. The 9th Duke of Marlborough ordered the piece for his American wife, Gladys, who he thought needed such jewels to "enter into society."*

50-54 Matching sapphires to create a sumptuous necklace is an increasingly difficult art. First the sapphires must match each other both in shade of color and in brilliance. Often the sapphires will be recut so that the table of each stone is of uniform proportions. Several sketches will be made as a rough guide for the craftsman. Each of the individual settings will be made to suit the exact height and width of the stone to be accommodated. Often, deep stones will be set deeper in a mounting to give an impression of uniformity. A necklace may be matched by sapphire earrings, a sapphire ring, and sometimes a sapphire bracelet; a magnificent suite sold by Sotheby's is shown here. Such suites can still occasionally be seen in leading London jewelers on Bond Street or in New York on Fifth Avenue. However, the reverse process—the breaking up of such pieces to provide gems for ring settings—is far more commonly the case today.

55 *A gem-quality Ceylon sapphire with a cornflower-blue shade. Here, undulating tapered baguettes, in the ballerina style, give the sapphire additional "life."*

56 (BELOW) *A Ceylon fancy color sapphire necklace. The term sapphire is used to refer to corundum in all colors and shades other than red. Yellow, purple, pink and green sapphires, as well as pastel shades, are imaginatively used in this piece of modern jewelry.*

Many Sri Lankans have the name of a gemstone as a personal name. Gems are not only a principal source of wealth to the country but, more importantly, are regarded as a protector of the island, in both a spiritual and a material sense. In recent years the Sri Lanka State Gem Corporation has been set up to rationalize the gem industry there. All stones shipped from that country are tested by the corporation's very able staff to prove their genuineness.

There have been wonderful finds recently of sapphires, as well as of rubies in Madagascar. While the sapphires tend to have a slightly purplish tinge to the blue, they are a welcome addition to the ever-dwindling supply of fine Ceylon and Burma stones—as well as, of course, the fact that the Kashmir mines, while yielding a very few stones now, are largely extinct.

The internal world of sapphires, that is, how the stones appear to a jeweler using a 10X loupe, or to a gemologists using a microscope, is indeed extraordinary. In *The Internal World of Gemstones,* Dr. Gübelin presents an extraordinary series of pictures of sapphire inclusions. In a Ceylon sapphire one can see the remnants of the crystallization pattern—a diary of the gem's growth. It is common to find a microscopic zircon inclusion surrounded by a brilliant halo. Often, in Ceylon and Burma stones, one can also observe a liquid lake with edges that resemble a feather. A sapphire from Burma, viewed under a microscope, can be seen to have within it densely woven criss-crossing rutile needles that are different in character from the rutile needles seen in a Ceylon sapphire. Finally, a Kashmir sapphire will have long bands of concentrated color that are colloidal suspensions of color arranged in parallel form.

Thus, while the gem connoisseur might say that a particular gem sapphire has a "Kashmir color," by viewing that stone under a microscope, one can, in fact, determine exactly where it crystallized. Inclusions in Cambodian sapphires often reveal a red crystal, free flowing as a meteor in space. Origin, that is to say, where the sapphire was mined, has come to be of immense importance. It's a bit like a Rembrandt painting: in the 1900s, a connoisseur's eyes, a renowned Rembrandt dealer, for example, might declare "This is a Rembrandt," and it was accepted as such. In the 1980s and 90s, increasingly, any sapphire of importance was accompanied by a certificate stating sapphire origin—Kashmir or Burma, or Ceylon, or Thai, for example.

It is a sign of the technological tenor of our times that very often a knowledgeable dealer, and certainly a neophyte, will look at the certificate before examining the gem. People increasingly feel more comfortable with a scientific determination that employs microscopic investigation of the internal world of the gemstone, coupled with precise spectrographic and fluorescent examination of the stone before looking at the gemstone with one's own eyes. It must be remembered, however, that the eye is an extraordinary scientific instrument in and of itself and that, if properly educated, can discern incredible numbers of shades of blue (and of red, green, and other colors).

The landscape of these inclusions is not only beautiful but important in enabling one to distinguish synthetic from genuine stones. Nature expresses itself in gemstones in straight lines. The presence of criss-crossing rutile needles, for example, is an indisputable sign of genuineness. Curved lines, on the other hand, invariably indicate that a stone has been created artificially. Similarly, included zircon crystals are also proof that a sapphire is genuine.

Recently, in the Far East, increasing numbers of sapphires have been subjected to heat-enhancement to improve their color. Although generally believed revolutionary, this process (a development of the last few years) is, in fact, an old gem cutters' trick. Tavernier noted that in seventeenth-century Ceylon, both rubies and sapphires were heat-treated in order to intensify their color.

In addition to being heated, a significantly large number of sapphires recently have been irradiated. Yellow sapphires, for example, having a watery, pale yellow cast, appear to be magnificently yellow after irradiation. While heat enhancement of sapphires is accepted by the gemological community as not interfering with the naturalness of the stone, irradiation of sapphires to improve their color (or irradiation of diamonds, for that matter) is not acceptable. Irradiated stones can fade over a period of months; heat-treated stones do not. Thus, to a connoisseur, irradiated stones are looked upon as synthetic and fetch very little money. Exposing a "possibly" irradiated sapphire to twenty-four hours of longwave ultraviolet light or to several days of sunlight will often cause the stone's color to fade noticeably if it has, indeed, been irradiated.

In Bangkok today enterprising Chinese merchants, who often love gambling, will place a sapphire inside an oven for what they call "cooking." Either the stone will crack or its color will change, sometimes becoming more intense, sometimes less intense. Just as there are different cooking styles for food in China, so, too, are there secret "recipes" and many different methods of "cooking" sapphires. These "cooked" stones are sold and accepted as genuine. Heating sapphires dulls the life of the stones. To the connoisseur, therefore, while the burnt sapphire might still be regarded as genuine, it is not quite as beautiful as an unheated sapphire. Sapphires that have been treated in this fashion will fluoresce slightly and exhibit tiny microscopic platelets.

These platelets appear almost as "cups and saucers" when viewed through a microscope. In the heating of the sapphire, the crystal (the cup) expands differentially and a tiny crack forms around it. There are often "cottony" inclusions that appear as hazy banding in the stone. These cotton inclusions are solid particles that have been reduced through the burning process—rutile needles and other included crystals. After burning, the sapphire will be bluer looking, but often will lose in brilliance and luster. It is estimated that more than 90 per cent of commercial sapphires today are heat treated. Sapphires of the very top quality are generally not heat treated because of the risk of damage.

As in the case of ruby, an inclusion in sapphire that is of particular interest is the presence of crossed rutile needles. When these hexagonal, crisscrossing needles in a stone are orientated correctly, the cabochon will exhibit a "star" when light from an outside source, either the sun or a flashlight, is shone upon the stone. A star Burma, or a star Ceylon, sapphire can be a most magnificent gem.

The supply of gem sapphires is dwindling most rapidly. Kashmir is exhausted, Burma is finished and Sri Lanka is declining rapidly as a production source. Estate-market jewelry—that is, pieces containing stones from previous generations—is being sought by auction houses and fine retail stores throughout the world.

When Marco Polo traveled to the East, he was able to sell sapphires to the Khan for, in his words, "twice the value." This phrase puzzled scholars at first. It is to be remembered, however, that it was in Marco Polo's day that we first hear of the creation and use of paper money. The Italian merchant, Polo, described the Khan's "alchemy" in creating paper money and in making sure that it was accepted, "upon pain of death," throughout the Khan's kingdom in China. Because the Mongol ruler would buy gems once a year and because he himself created paper currency as a means of exchange, it is not surprising that he was willing to settle with Marco Polo by paying him "twice the value" in that form.

Paper currency continued into the fifteenth century in Ming China. An explosion in inflation at that time caused the Chinese people to refuse to accept this currency, a refusal that lasted for five hundred years. This conflict between the value of paper currency and gems is similar to the situation in the world gem markets today.

In order to see what a gem sapphire truly looks like, one can visit a fine retail store or a museum. At the Smithsonian Institution, the Bismarck Sapphire is of magnificent size and quality. There are intensely colored, faceted sapphires as well as engraved gems on display in the jewelry collection room at the Victoria and Albert Museum, London. In the Musée National d'Histoire Naturelle in Paris, the extremely fine 132-carat Raspoli Sapphire, dating from the time of Louis XIV, has survived.

The word "sapphire," *sapir* in Hebrew, is a synonym for *sippur*, Hebrew for story. Mystical Jews used the word *sefirot* to denote the emanations of God in the universe. Sapphires have always been regarded as the secret message from beyond. The Persians even believed that the world rested on a giant sapphire, and that the reflection of this stone colored the entire universe. Connoisseurs of sapphire would all agree that sapphire, when it is of gem quality, gives the viewer a sense of peace, of infinity and of magnificent beauty.

THREE

EMERALD

"In Manta, a seacoast province of Peru, was a people that worshipped a giant emerald that was said to be as big as an ostrich egg. On important feast days it was taken from the temple and shown to the people, among whom were throngs of Indians who had come from a great distance to worship the stone and offer up sacrifices of smaller emeralds. The priests and the Cacique of Manta had persuaded these poor people that small emeralds were the daughters of the big emerald and, therefore, no other offering would be so well received. This selfish ploy had permitted them to accumulate in Manta an incomparable treasure of emeralds, that was discovered during the Peruvian conquest by Pedro de Alvarado and his companions, among whom was my father, Garcilaso de la Vega."

The Royal Commentaries of Garcilaso the Inca

EMERALDS ARE THE magical link between the eye and the deepest recesses of the earth. Unlike ruby or sapphire, which are generally carried by rivers from their original source, emeralds are recovered *in situ*. There is a magnificent pre-Columbian Chimú mask in the Mujica Gallo collection in Peru that touches on the enduring mystery of emerald. The mask, a nobleman's face to eternity, is primarily of gold—its color reminiscent of the sun, the sacred center of American Indian culture; and from the eye-sockets emerald beads peer out, regenerating themselves with the help of the light from the sun and serving as a symbolic association between the dead warrior and his rebirth in the hereafter.

The ancient Egyptians also regarded emerald, with its deep green color unlike the green of anything else known to them, as being mystical and magical. As far back as the nineteenth century BC, in the XIIth Dynasty (Middle Kingdom), emeralds were used in funerary jewelry for dead nobles. The problem, however, was that emeralds were in such short supply in Egypt that to compensate for their scarcity, green faience came to be used—skillfully simulating the majesty of emerald color.

In the first century BC, a major seam of emerald was discovered, running parallel to the Red Sea at Jebel Zubara, in Egypt. Although the emeralds were highly included with whitish veins, and their luster was not specially exciting, they were sought because of their greenness. The historian Pliny describes how wealthy Romans would vie to wear quantities of emerald jewelry: rings, necklaces and earrings. At that time, however, they were not able to facet emeralds; the art of faceting was understood only from the fifteenth century, and before that emerald was either cut in cabochon form or left in its natural crystal (hexagonal) shape. Just as when the Egyptians did not have enough emeralds to go around, they took to imitating them, so too did the Romans, modeling green glass in hexagonal shapes. As such, these are early examples of imitation emeralds. It is not unlikely that in ancient Rome such hexagonally shaped green "stones" were sold to unsuspecting buyers as the real thing.

In the late Renaissance a startling thing happened to the Western conception of beauty in an emerald. Stumbling upon the Inca and the Aztec wealth, primarily in the form of gold and emeralds, the Spanish conquistadors stunned Europe and the world with the beauty of the emeralds, mined originally in Colombia, which they sent from America. There was an extensive trade in these gems throughout Southern and Central America, which the Spaniards came to dominate. Garcilaso de la Vega (c. 1535–1616), son of an Inca princess and a Spanish conquistador, wrote an account of events before and during the actual conquest of Peru, in which he detailed the journey through South America in search of emeralds. The passage quoted above is taken from this source.

How did the Spaniards—and how do we—judge whether an emerald is a gemstone? An emerald is a complex combination of beryllium-aluminum silicate (beryl), in its pure state a colorless crystal. When tiny traces of chromium are added in nature to this beryl, it becomes green and is termed emerald. Beryl also occurs in other colors such as purplish red (morganite) or blue (aquamarine), resulting from the presence of other impurities. Aluminum silicate itself is quite rare. The juxtaposition of chromium with it, however, occurs in extremely few places—hence, the great rarity of emeralds.

Slight differences in the amount of chromium will alter radically the depth of green in emerald. Within the green shade of emerald are worlds of difference. The finest green, which is seen in stones from a specific mine in Colombia, is called "old mine" green. Such stones are found in the Muzo mine. When the Spanish conquistador, Gonzalo Jiménez de Quesada, tortured the Indians and was thus able to discover the site of the Chivor mine, the Spaniards reasoned that there should be more emerald mines nearby. In 1567, after incalculable human toil and effort, the Muzo mine was discovered. The Muzo site is torrid, jungle-like and inaccessible. The air can hardly be breathed. Each section of the mine had to be cleared by hand because the use of explosives would have destroyed the fragile emerald crystals. The finds, however, were breathtaking: deep-green, gem emerald crystals. The emeralds that were wrested greedily from the earth were sent all over the world by the Spaniards, but the finest ones did not go to Spain. Gems tend to find their way, of course, to the highest bidder, and the highest bidders in the late sixteenth and early seventeenth centuries were to be found in India. There, maharajas and maharanis would pay fabulous sums for precious stones. The superfine Muzo "old mine" stones were also called "Chibcha stones," after the Colombian Indian people, and generally were rounded into "pebbles," drilled and worn as necklaces.

The second-finest shade of green emerald is to be found in stones from the original Chivor mine. This shade tends to have more blue than the Muzo shade. To some neophytes the Chivor blue-green stones appear, at first sight, to have more warmth and fire. The Muzo stones often appear to be over-dark or to have a hint of yellow in them. After exploiting the mines of Chivor and Muzo for several years, the Spaniards were no longer able to wrest important stones from the ground, and both mines were abandoned and lost sight of. In 1895 Muzo was rediscovered, and in 1904 Chivor was re-opened by Fritz Klein, an Idar-Oberstein gem dealer. None of the recently mined emeralds from Colombia can compare in their depth of color to that of the "old mine" stones which were shipped throughout the world before the seventeenth century.

It takes many years of comparing shades of green to develop connoisseurship in emeralds. Although some connoisseurs occasionally will prefer the Chivor blue-green to the Muzo yellowish-green, the Colombian emerald is unanimously regarded as the finest in the world. Aside from the Colombian (and the Egyptian) mines, emeralds have been found in Russia, India and Africa. In 1832, in the Ural Mountains of Russia, a seam of emeralds was discovered. After the discovery, quite a few jewelry pieces were made containing Russian emeralds, which, while somewhat light in color, were relatively free from inclusions. These Russian mines have by now stopped yielding the purer emeralds, the material produced today being extremely opaque and generally uninteresting. In 1945, near Ajmer, in northwestern India, emerald deposits were discovered, but these, too, were disappointing in the amount of output. The great hope for an abundant and top-quality emerald supply has been Africa. In 1955, in Rhodesia (now Zimbabwe), prospectors looking for lithium stumbled upon a fabulous find of emeralds. They sent the first specimens to Dr. Gübelin for testing, informing the gemologists that they intended to call the new find "vulcan emeralds." Dr. Gübelin, however, urged a name change, based on the site of the prospectors' base camp—Sandawana—and the stones from there have been called "Sandawana emeralds" ever since. The sizes of the stones tended to be well under a carat; their color was a less intense green than that of Colombian stones, but because of their brilliance, the African stones were much sought after by jewelry manufacturers and jewelry makers. Small Sandawana emeralds were used for bracelets, pins and cluster rings. The emeralds had tremendous life and were reasonably priced.

Within twenty years of the commencement of mining, however, Sandawana output fell considerably. Because the stones were small, Sandawana emeralds did not at any time succeed in taking over the premier position in the emerald world. Emeralds from a second African source, Zambia, started to appear on the market in the 1970s. Slightly blackish in overtone and often highly included, they, too, were sought after for the "commercial" end of the emerald field. Because the shade of green lacked the crispness and warmth of Colombian emeralds, Zambian emeralds (often superbly cut in Israel) also do not compete seriously with the gem South African material. Despite this, however, there are a few very fine Zambian stones.

Brazil, finally, is another important source of emeralds. The Brazilian stones tend not to have the peppery inclusions common to African emeralds. The material, however, is very opaque. Brazilian lapidaries are extremely skilled and are able to cut the material so that a Brazilian emerald is often very well proportioned and, at first glance, quite attractive. A frequent problem, however, is that there are many open veins in Brazilian crystals.

Of critical importance in judging a Colombian, Zambian, Brazilian, or in fact, an emerald from any area, is the degree to which the emerald has been oiled or, in many cases, impregnated with opticon. As with the heat enhancement of ruby and sapphire, in the 1990s, great strides were made in oiling emerald rough before it was cut. Sometimes, "heavy amounts of oiling" was added, and, to the gem connoisseur, generally, heavy oiling is considered a great detriment to the value and quality of the emerald. Opticon, which is a binding substance that seeps into the pores or veins of the stone, is considered a alter-

57 *A wonderfully matched set of pear-shaped emeralds highlighted by a sinuous line of baguettes and round diamonds.*

58 Rough emerald in a crystal matrix. Emerald in calcite can be mined only by labor-intensive processes. Explosives would shatter the fragile emerald crystals. In Colombia, emerald-mining techniques have barely changed since the days of the Spanish conquistadors.

59 A pyrite inclusion in a Colombian emerald from the Chivor mine. This beautiful included crystal of pyrite, visible tinder a microscope, indicates that Chivor stones have a history of hydrothermal crystallization.

60 (ABOVE) A three-phase inclusion; under a microscope, a characteristic jagged outline containing a rounded gas bubble and a square crystal can be detected in the interior of almost all Colombian emeralds. Thus, a three-phase inclusion is proof that an emerald is both genuine and that it originated in Colombia.

61 An inclusion in a synthetic emerald. This veil-like inclusion, as revealed under a microscope, is evidence that the emerald is synthetic. Color differences between genuine and synthetic emeralds are the basis for a secondary test; examination under a microscope for internal inclusions is much more important.

62 *A gem Colombian emerald; this fine stone, which contains a trace of black, is from the Muzo mine. Its translucency is great and it is an "old mine" gem. Although the stone is described as being "clean," all emeralds have inclusions, and here a tiny inclusion is visible just beneath the lower crown facet.*

63 *A Chivor Colombian emerald. The green of this stone has more than a touch of blue in it, resulting in a sense of coolness that is much prized by emerald connoisseurs.*

64 *This group of three gems all from one estate piece match each other in color texture. These stones are "old mine" emeralds found in the sixteenth century.*

65 Two emeralds viewed from different angles. Often, one can observe the color of an emerald even more clearly by turning the stone over so that it rests on its table (top facet).

66 Sandawana emeralds of a very beautiful green color. These stones were discovered in Rhodesia in 1955. Although of good color and relatively free from inclusions, individual Sandawana stones tend to be under a carat and thus the supply from this recently discovered source has not quenched the increasing worldwide demand for gem emeralds.

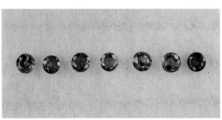

67 Zambian emeralds of commercial quality, discovered in 1974. Newly discovered emeralds in Zambia often display a crispness and liveliness. There is, however, an overlay of blackishness to their color, which has prevented Zambia from replacing Colombia as the prime source of gem emeralds.

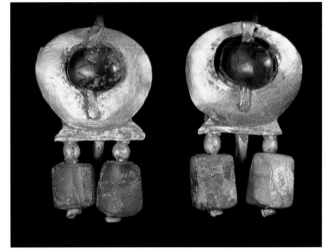

68 (ABOVE) *A Hellenistic emerald ring of the second century* BC; *this magnificent ring in the form of a snake was probably intended for amuletic purposes.*

69 (ABOVE, RIGHT) *Roman sapphire and emerald earrings; in Roman times sapphires and rubies were cur in cabochon form, while emeralds were left in their original crystal shapes and simply drilled. Egyptian emeralds do not bear comparison with the later-discovered Colombian emeralds, which possess nor only fine color but also translucency.*

70 *A Roman necklace with emerald beads from Egypt. Open gold work in this cut-out form is called opus interrasile and contrasts pleasingly with the solidity of the emerald.*

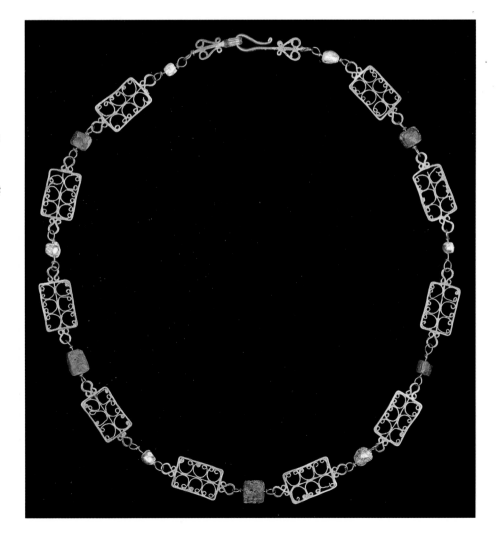

71 Crown, designed and made in 1967 by Pierre Arpels of Paris for the Empress Farah Diba, wife of Mohammed Reza Pahlavi, Shah of Iran. A total of 1,646 stones from the Royal Treasury were used in the creation of this crown; they include diamonds, pearls, spinels and, as a principal feature, two large emeralds. The stones in the former royal collection in Tehran are considered to be the most precious assemblage of emeralds in the world.

72 A belt-buckle in the former royal collection in Iran; the emerald weighs 175 carats and originally came from Colombia in the sixteenth century. Emeralds mined then were both larger in size and deeper and more organic in color than stones being mined anywhere in the world today.

73-74 *A very fine "old mine" Muzo yellowish-green emerald set in a ring. This stone was first cut centuries ago in India, probably in cabochon form; it was later altered to an emerald-cut shape and mounted in the early twentieth century. The side view shows the style of setting in a ring "sculptured" to make it beautiful from every visible angle—the top (bezel) or the sides (shank).*

75 *An 18th century emerald ring with an emerald cut in a rose cut fashion to imitate the "rose cut" diamonds of the period.*

76 (FAR RIGHT) *Emeralds were cut in a cabochon form before the sixteenth century; in this ring a gem-quality emerald cabochon of deep-green color is exactly matched by a gem-quality Burma ruby. Cabochons tend to emphasize a stone's color and luster, but such stones are never as brilliant as a faceted gem.*

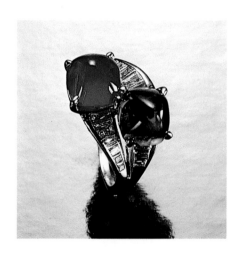

77, 78 *A modern cabochon emerald ring by Philip Zowine that is reminiscent of both medieval Islamic and medieval Western rings. Here, an "old mine" emerald is gracefully mounted in the yellow stirrup-shaped shank so as to emphasize its extraordinary height.*

79 Mughal-style nineteenth-century Indian earrings and an eighteenth- to nineteenth-century Indian-inspired bracelet, both containing small emeralds. Indian jewelry is characterized by the vibrant mixing of diamonds, pearls, rubies or red enamel, and emeralds. These color combinations also occur in Renaissance and later European jewelry.

80 (BELOW) Detail of an old Jaipur Indian necklace. Increasingly in the Bombay market today, old Indian necklaces containing emerald beads are being broken up. Each bead will then be sliced to yield two fine emeralds which can in turn be faceted. These are sold to international gem merchants and are eventually mounted in modern settings.

81, 82 Part of an eighteenth-century Georgian suite of emerald jewelry. In the eighteenth century naturalistic motifs were imaginatively combined with lively emeralds. The detail shows a dragonfly resting on an open flower.

83 *A suite consisting of bracelet, necklace and ring. Such matching sets of jewlery would be almost impossible to assemble today. Each emerald had to be not only color matched but also to be recut so as to fit in with the entire ensemble. Many pieces such as these are now broken up to yield individual stones for ring settings.*

84 The value of this emerald and diamond necklace would be based primarily on its large octagonal emerald. All the diamonds it contains are "old mine" and would have to be recut (cf. ill. 101). Although the color of the emeralds is indifferent, their brilliance melds well with that of the diamonds.

85 *A Chimú, pre-Columbian gold mask with emerald "eyes," from northern Peru. For the Chimú both gold and emerald had important symbolic significance.*

86 *A pre-Columbian gold stylized figure of a turtle from Panama (Cochlé culture), incorporating an emerald—one of the few surviving pre-Columbian pieces containing an original emerald. Almost all the treasures of the Incas were melted down by the Spaniards for their gold content, the emeralds being prised out and shipped off to India or to Europe.*

ation of the material. Virtually all fine emeralds are accompanied with a certificate describing the degree, if any, of oiling or the addition of opticon to the material. (*see Documntary Illustrations* pp. 238–239).

The process of oiling, indeed, has been known for centuries in India. There, balsam wood oil, a very permanent oil, was classically added to emeralds during the cutting process and is considered to be of much less significance than the more modern oiling techniques.

In the case of Brazilian emeralds, a stone with open veins may sometimes be oiled to improve its color. The tremendous bargains that one may be tempted to buy from a "street" gem merchant in Rio de Janeiro often lose their color as the oil gradually evaporates over the years.

Few of the other known locations for emerald is of commercial importance. It is true that isolated emeralds can be found in North Carolina (United States), in Austria and in Norway, but these have been uniformly of medium and poorer quality. For gem emerald one must always turn to Colombia.

Aside from their color-shade differences, Colombian emeralds can be subdivided also on the basis of their inclusion. It is possible to determine, with the aid of a microscope, from which particular mine—Muzo, Chivor Cosquez, Gachalá—an emerald comes. Aside from the yellow shade of green that is common to most Muzo emeralds, Dr. Gübelin points out, in *The Internal World of Gemstones*, that under 100X magnification, the presence of a yellow-brown inclusion called "parasite" definitely indicates a Muzo origin. Peering into a Muzo stone under the microscope or with a jeweler's loupe, one often can see a pool of swirling color, deep yellow-green in nature, with tiny square boxes of calcite swimming alongside these yellow-brown crystals of parasite. This organic effect has been called *jardin* by French jewelers. Anybody who expects to find a flawless emerald will always be disappointed. Under 10X magnification every emerald that I have studied has revealed some inclusion. The Chivor stones, aside from their bluish cast of color, often reveal, under a microscope, a brilliantly lit, golden-faceted ball of pyrite crystal. Occasionally, a Muzo stone will have a pyrite crystal, but pyrite is usually suggestive of Chivor origin. Colombian emeralds generally will contain a three-phase inclusion. This is a peculiarly "jagged island" containing a round shape that is a gas bubble and a square that is a solid inclusion. Upon seeing a three-phase inclusion, one can be certain that the emerald indeed "grew up" in the hydrothermal conditions of Colombia. These inclusions also indicate that the emerald is genuine.

There are vast numbers of synthetically grown emeralds, produced by various processes. The Gilson and Chatham methods are two of the processes used. Under magnification the synthetic stones often reveal veil-like and wispy inclusions, occasionally gas bubbles and jagged tubes. Color is not a good means of distinguishing synthetic from genuine emeralds because, occasionally, something close to the subtle green shade of a natural stone will be observed in a synthetic emerald. Synthetics tend to be much freer from inclusions than their genuine counterparts.

Newcomers to the world of emeralds are curious about the effect that the widespread existence of synthetic emeralds has on the value of genuine emeralds. How can a genuine emerald be so highly valued when an often purer and larger synthetic stone is sold for a fraction of the price? Firstly, after a lengthy education, a connoisseur is able to notice metallic nuances in the color of synthetic emeralds so that, in practice, the experienced eye can determine that the color of such stones tends to have a "manufactured" look. Secondly, stones can be submitted readily to a local gemological laboratory where, for a fairly minimal fee, a certificate will be issued attesting to whether a particular emerald is genuine. Thus, while synthetic emeralds have been on the market for at least forty years, the price differences between the genuine and the synthetic have increased markedly. At auction ten-carat emeralds have fetched over $50,000 per carat, while a comparable synthetic emerald will often sell for only hundreds of dollars for the entire stone.

Where does one look for fine emeralds today? One retraces the steps in the history of emerald. First of all, there are the sources themselves, in Colombia and Africa. The Colombian gem mines—Muzo, Chivor, Cosquez and Gachalá—are at present still yielding emeralds. After hundreds of years of being tapped, however, the mines are producing emeralds that are smaller and less fine in color than stones recovered in the past. The newly mined stones simply do not compare to the "old mine" pieces. Because of the great value of emeralds and because of political uncertainty in the outlying regions of the country, the mines are at present under the control of the Colombian Army.

Rough emeralds are purchased by gem merchants and then cut either in Colombia proper or in India. In the Bombay market one can see newly cut emerald pieces from Colombia in addition to the hand-me-downs of Indian maharajas and maharanis. These hand-me-downs, of course, are always of much greater interest to the gem connoisseur than are the newly mined stones. "Old mine" stones were originally sent to India via the Philippines, and even today in the Far East emerald is still called the "Filipino stone." These "old mine" stones were treasured for hundreds of years in the royal courts. For an idea of the richness of this emerald material, one need only look at the collection of the former crown jewels of Iran, now held (as collateral to back the nation's currency) in the Bank Melli in Tehran. This collection was originally in Delhi in 1739. After a brief period in Afghanistan, the gems were captured by the Persians. Boxes and boxes of emeralds in their rounded and tumbled forms can be seen. Also, studding crowns and belt-buckles, huge emeralds adorn pieces of royal jewelry. One almost never sees emeralds of this quality for sale at auction today.

The finest emerald object in the world is a little box—measuring 2 1/2 X 2 inches—fashioned entirely of emerald and diamond. The top of the box contains a 35-carat blue-green emerald of exquisite depth of color. Perfectly matched emeralds line all sides of the box. The box's original function is not clear. Whatever its use, for medicine or for jewels, it is undeniably of sumptuous richness.

The Topkapi Museum in Istanbul also has a collection similar to the crown jewels of Iran, but not quite as fine. Displayed in the American Museum of Natural History, New York, is a very fine emerald crystal, the Patricia Emerald, which is an example of "old mine" emerald rough. In the Green Vault in Dresden there is a figure of a Moor holding a plate on which is resting a group of emerald crystals. This was a gift to the Elector of Saxony in the sixteenth century. It symbolizes in graphic terms the riches of the New World–emeralds offered by a native to a European monarch. The piece itself is a masterpiece of goldsmithing work. It took Balthasar Permoser fourteen years to fashion. In the Smithsonian in Washington, the Spanish Inquisition Necklace contains a fabulous group of faceted emerald barrel-shaped beads; each bead is drilled and is strung with Indian diamonds from Golconda. The depth of Muzo green and the purity of these emerald gems is extraordinary. There are very fine faceted emeralds in the Townsend collection in the Victoria and Albert Museum. A 35-carat, cushion-shaped stone may be seen in the Smithsonian. African emeralds, with their more recent history, have not yet found their way in significant numbers into museum cases. Because of the decline in Colombian production, however, there is no doubt that the African stones will also be on view for the gem connoisseur some day.

Down the centuries connoisseurs have attributed differing qualities to emeralds. The Roman Emperor Nero, it is said, would watch gladiatorial contests through an emerald crystal and be calmed. The Spanish conqueror of Peru, Francisco Pizarro, upon seeing the emerald treasures of the Incas, was driven mad in his search for "El Dorado" and his quest for more emeralds. Where is the most beautiful emerald in the world today? Perhaps still waiting to be rediscovered. As Garcilaso de la Vega wrote in 1581 about the fabulous wonder of pre-Columbian Peru:

> As for the giant emerald, it had disappeared well before the Spaniards arrived. Indeed, the Indians who hid it did it so successfully that it has never been found since, no more than have many other treasures that were buried in the same earth.

FOUR

WHITE DIAMOND

> "Kissing your hand may make you feel very, very good,
> but a diamond and sapphire bracelet lasts forever."
>
> —ANITA LOOS, *Gentlemen Prefer Blondes*

N THE *Ratna Pariska*, written in the Gupta period (sixth century) in India, the qualities of the perfect diamond are described: it should have "six sharp points, eight very flat and similar sides, twelve straight and sharp edges." In addition, the stone should have a pure transparency, clarity and be perfectly white (i.e. colorless). In other words, the diamond should be in the form of an absolutely colorless and perfectly shaped octahedral crystal. In *The History of Diamond Production and the Diamond Trade*, Godehard Lenzen quotes an Indian connoisseur of the Gupta period as saying:"If a diamond possesses all these qualities, it is to be desired above all other jewels."

Until the fifteenth century man's knowledge of how to facet diamonds was imperfect. Consequently, a diamond was an *objet trouvé*, and it would be mounted (in the form in which it was found in the rivers of central India and often sold in Golconda) as an octahedral crystal set in a ring. Indian Lapidaries (manuscripts concerned with the qualities of precious stones) described nuances of color and grading systems for diamond imperfections. These writings are remarkably similar to modern-day Antwerp and American how-to-evaluate-diamond books. In its system for grading the shades of white diamonds, described below, the Gemological Institute of America (GIA) echoes the old Indian system of differentiating four grades of color.

For the Indians, a perfectly pure and completely white diamond would have the "magical" property of dividing white light into all the spectral colors. In the Indian

73

cosmology light would be dispersed into a rainbow. In *Diamonds—Myth, Magic and Reality*, Lenzen states that this property was so important that only Brahmins were allowed to possess these pure, colorless diamonds. If a diamond had a hint of yellow in it, landowners could purchase it. Highly off-color yellow stones were allotted to merchants (the Vaisya class). Finally, the darkish black diamonds were allocated to the working man (the Sutra class) and to members of the warrior class (Kshatriya). Any large stones of pure quality had to be offered first, however, to the ruler of Golconda, and as a result hardly any diamonds of gem quality found their way to Europe before the year 1000.

The Roman martial view of diamonds stressed not the sensibility to dispersion—the magic rainbow—but to the hardness, or adamantine quality, of diamonds, which were believed to be able to break iron. To the practical mind of the Chinese, diamonds were treasured for their utilitarian engraving ability. It is only after diamonds had come to be successfully faceted and polished in medieval times that the history of their being sought after as purely aesthetic objects begins.

In the fourteenth century a remarkable technological breakthrough occurred, probably in Europe but possibly in the East. A diamond cutter was able either to cleave (slice a crystal along an axis plane) or to place the pointed termination of an octahedral crystal against a turning wheel and in so doing, he ground the point of the diamond one-third of the way down to the girdle of the crystal. The flat top of the table formed a rectangle. The ideal proportion of the rectangle would conform to Pythagorean golden mean proportions, and because of their squarish tops, such stones came to be called "table-cut" diamonds. This type of cut was the first step in releasing the brilliance and fire inherent in a diamond crystal. Until the stage was reached when table-cut diamonds could be faceted, ruby and emerald were considered more valuable than diamond. As it became possible to make diamonds more brilliant, however, their value rose greatly in comparison with their rival gems. In the Renaissance table cuts were replaced by rose cuts and the Mazarin cut. Finally, in the early 1900s, Marcel Tolkowski, a mathematician and engineer who grew up in Antwerp, established a very accurate system for maximizing the return of white light to the observer's eye (brilliance) and the splitting of light into many colors (dispersion or "fire") in a round brilliant cut. Tolkowski found that if a diamond was cut very precisely, with the crown angles at 34.5° and the pavilion angles at 40.75°, and if the table occupied 53 per cent of the width of the stone, then the optical properties of the stone would be seen to their best advantage. Thus, the diamond, for centuries regarded as an object of magic and sacred beauty, has in recent times become the object of precise scientific calibration to be processed by advanced technological means. As such, it represents a paradigm of human thought over the last two thousand years, and constitutes—in every sense—the riches of the earth.

After Tavernier had visited the Golconda mines in 1661, he wrote:

> The first time I was at this mine, there were nearly sixty-thousand working there, including men, women and children, who were employed in diverse ways, the men in digging, the women and children in carrying earth, for they search for the stones at this mine. . . .

Tavernier went on to describe the religious offerings that would take place once the mining site was selected:

> The place being thus prepared, all who are about to engage in the search assemble—men, women and children, together with their employer and a party of his relatives and his friends. He brings with him a figure in stone of the god whom they worship, which is placed standing on the ground, and each person prostrates himself three times before it . . .

The prayers were thought to appease the mine spirits for the disturbance to the underground kingdom of diamonds. After this propitiatory offering, workers would excavate to a depth of up to fourteen feet and wash the clay, searching for diamonds. The original source of these alluvial diamonds, somewhere in bedrock near Hyderabad, has never been found. The very finest of the stones that were purchased by the ruler of Golconda, with his right of first refusal, were hidden in the palace treasury. Eventually, some of these superfine diamonds would pass through Tavernier's hands after the maharaja began to tire of them. Tavernier would buy them and resell them to Louis XIV of France. Tavernier's line drawings of fabulous diamonds (*see* p. 236) constitute the first detailed inventory of important gems. Among these were the Hope Diamond, the Darya-i-Nur and Nur-ul-'Ain, all historical colored diamonds (see next chapter).

After sixteen hundred years of dredging, however, the Indian mines became exhausted, though very recently electrifying news has leaked out of India that, once again, the Golconda mines are producing isolated, but in some cases, beautiful Golconda material, an amazing Renaissance. To return to the eighteenth century, however, just in time, in 1730, a new source of diamonds was discovered—in Brazil. These mines, much less vast than their Indian counterparts, lasted in quantity for only one hundred years, but again, as diamond dealers' luck would have it, when the Brazilian mines started to become exhausted in 1888, South African sources were discovered. Unlike their Indian and Brazilian predecessors, De Beers Consolidated Mines could increasingly employ labor-saving, heavy-duty machinery, and this has transformed diamond recovery into a capital-intensive industry. Five tons of rock have to be dug, moved, sorted and processed in order to yield a single one-carat gem diamond. When considering that a carat is $\frac{1}{142}$ of an ounce (200 mg), one realizes what a technological feat is involved here. Russia has gone even one step further. In desolate parts of Siberia, between the Yenisey and the Lena rivers, diamonds are extracted on a year-round, round-the-clock basis. Temperatures there are often as low as −20° and −60° Fahrenheit—the most adverse conditions in any of the world's diamond mines.

Not only have diamond production methods changed markedly over the years, but the ways of looking at a diamond—the modes of perception—have changed. In India, and in ancient China, the religious concept of the "diamond body" was what gave diamond its allure. The diamond itself, a symbol of the clarity and the purity of the "Brahma," was most important. In Europe at the time of the Renaissance, however, the diamond as a stone became subservient to the design of an entire piece of jewelry. A fine example of that period is the Canning Jewel, in the Victoria and Albert Museum. It is a piece containing a torso-shaped baroque pearl, and is made more brilliant through the addition of diamonds and rubies. Diamonds are used in the Canning Jewel to provide a color contrast with the gaiety of ruby and of the accompanying blue and green enameling.

More recently, around the turn of the century, diamonds were used as a kind of technical *tour de force*. Cartier created elaborately worked necklaces, bracelets and brooches, utilizing intricate settings. Seen from either the front or the back, each piece revealed a high level of craftsmanship. Each diamond had to be set separately and hundreds of production hours went into the creation of each piece. Since the 1960s we have come, curiously enough, back to the Indian view of the diamond, that is to say, to appreciate the diamond's quality, in and of itself. All too often, the settings for diamonds today are simple "Tiffany" settings, merely four prongs gripping the diamond itself. A certificate, which often accompanies an important diamond, is integral to our way of viewing the stone. Sometimes the diamond is not even set. It is sold merely in a diamond paper and sometimes only its certificate may

87, 88 The earliest diamond ring known. Roman,
third-century AD. The diamond crystal was mined
in the Indian diamond mines. The uncut crystal
was send to Rome and set into a bold design. The
Romans called diamond adamas—unconquerable.
As can be seen from the profile, the diamond's
power was thought to flow into the wearer, and the
pointed end of the diamond could cut glass and
other materials.

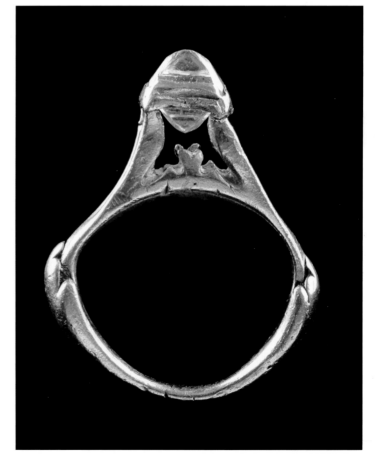

89 Diamond rough. Diamond rough recovered from rivers and alluvial mines such as those that formerly existed in India or in Venezuela will contain many rounded shapes and very few octahedral crystals. Rough can occur in all colors and often a poor exterior skin may cover a completely white interior. Venezuelan material, for example, tends to have a greenish skin, posing an additional challenge to the buyer and the evaluator of rough stones.

90 Trigons under high-power magnification. These tiny pits on the surface of the stone point in the direction of cleavage.

91 Different shapes in cut diamonds. The eventual shape of a diamond depends upon the original rough crystal. In the United States round brilliant cuts tend to be most popular. All other shapes are called "fancies."

92 Diamond rough crystal in an octahedral form. A perfect crystal such as this will have relatively little wastage in cutting, and yield the largest possible cut stone.

93 (FAR RIGHT) A diamond in cleavage form, a type often found in rivers. The Cullinan Diamond was one such stone (cf. ill. 23).

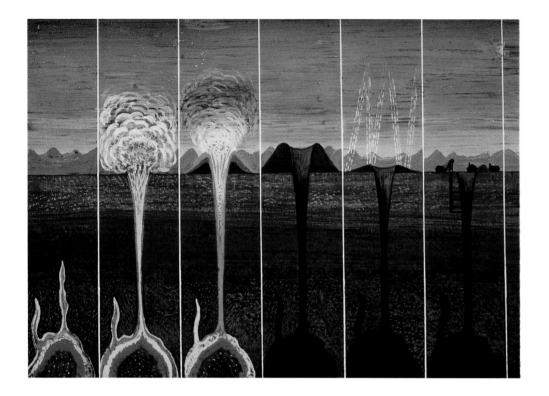

94 (ABOVE) The geological origin of the diamond starts deep within the earth. Diamonds formed under high pressure are forced toward the earth's surface in Kimberlite pipes.

95 Diamonds in rough form being graded for size, color and purity at De Beers. There are over three thousand separate classifications for rough.

96 Placing a diamond on the wheel. This operation always carries an element of risk: diamond dust is sprinkled on the wheel and abrades the diamond.

97 The successive cutting stages of a rough diamond crystal to a fully brilliant trilliant shape. The skill of the diamond cutter is to yield the largest size and most brilliant gem from these interpenetrated flat crystals.

98 (LEFT) *An 18th-century giardinetti ring showing an octahedral pointed diamond, table-cut diamonds, as well as rose-cut and old mine cuts.*

99 (RIGHT) *A perfectly limpid "portrait" diamond. Mined and cut in India in the early 18th century. Portrait diamonds were placed above miniature portraits in Renaissance rings. Note how one can see the shank of the ring so clearly.*

100 (LEFT) *An engraved diamond from the early nineteenth century. Because of the hardness of the material, the engraving of diamonds is exceptionally difficult. The bear may symbolize the Swiss city of Berne.*

101 (RIGHT) *A fine "old mine" diamond with a high crown and small table which emphasized luster (the splitting of light in prismatic colors) in the platinum ring, Edwardian, c. 1910, English.*

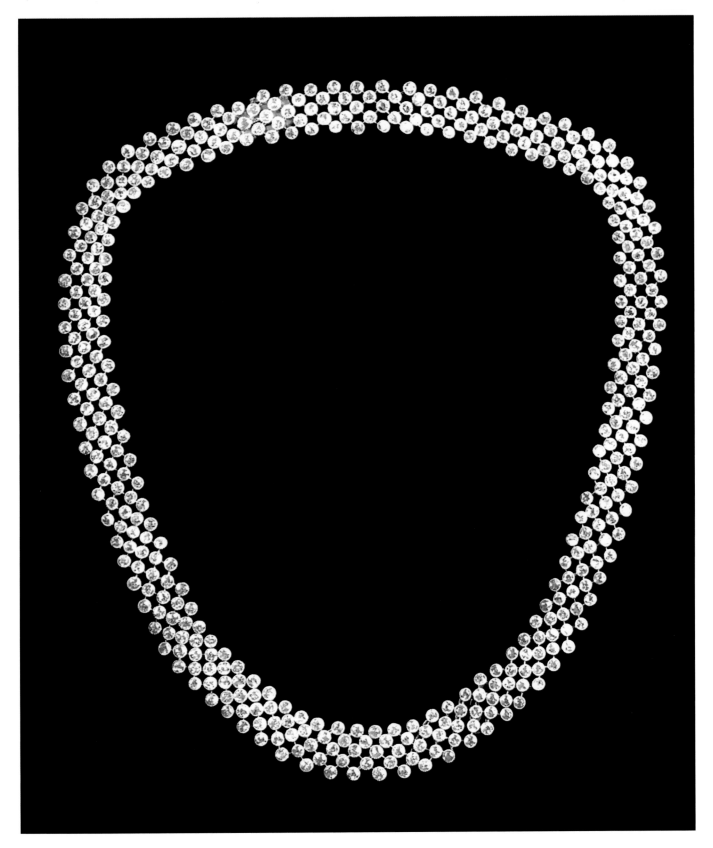

102 *A finely-crafted diamond necklace made by Chaumet, c. 1910, in platinum. This necklace is extra-ordinarily flexible, each link being connected with its neighbor through multiple linkages, and nests perfectly on the wearer's neck.*

103 The Canning Jewel, a Renaissance pendant designed around a natural baroque pearl. The craftsman who created this piece contrasted the lustrous white pearl with cabochon rubies and green enameling. Set into the forehead of the Triton is a Golconda octahedral diamond crystal, pointed toward the heavens and symbolically transmitting supernatural powers to the god of the sea.

be examined most carefully. In order to understand this "certificate craze," one must first examine the diamond itself.

The quality of diamond, which is composed of pure crystallized carbon, is based on color, clarity, cutting proportions and carat weight. Color is the most important distinguishing characteristic of the first three parameters. If a diamond contains more than one atom of nitrogen in one hundred thousand of carbon, the stone will have a slightly yellowish color.

During the 1950s the GIA developed a system of grading diamonds. Until then, diamonds had been termed "River" if they were of high color (very white). River diamonds were those of alluvial origin as opposed to diamonds found in situ. The second and third degrees of whiteness were termed "Top Wesselton" and "Wesselton," respectively, after the Wesselton mine at Kimberley which tended to yield diamonds characterized by a very faint yellow tinge. Lower grades would be "Top Crystal," "Crystal" and, finally, "Cape" stones, the last being noticeably yellowish. Under the GIA system, perfectly white stones are called "D" color, the next less white, "E" color, and so on until at "J" color a stone looks yellowish to the eye. This sequence of coloring continues as far as "Z" color (see also next chapter). By splitting the River grade into two colors, "D" and "E," and the Top Wesselton into two colors, "F" and "G," a more precise standard of separation was set. At first, traditional diamond dealers resisted the introduction of this system. Not only had the familiar appellation "River" lasted seventy years, but the introduction of "D" and "E" seemed an unnecessary "splitting of hairs."

The GIA determines a diamond's color grading with the aid of controlled conditions created in a light-box using artificial, non-fluorescent light. It is calibrated to match "Northern light" exactly. For centuries, before the invention of the light-box, diamond dealers had been able to sort diamonds and make value judgments based only on viewing them by Northern light on a reasonably clear day. Northern light is very distinctive and soft, and has a slight aura of blue to it. Vermeer captures this quality in his paintings, suffusing his silent figures in an ethereal glow of blue-white light. The light that diamond dealers consider true Northern light is the light as experienced in Antwerp and in Holland, where many of the fine diamond connoisseurs originally came from. By artificially duplicating this Low Country light, the GIA has enabled diamond sorting to continue at night or in any working conditions.

A diamond to be graded is placed, table down, in the light-box. Inside the box, arranged like resting soldiers, are perhaps six or seven other pre-graded diamonds, one of D color, followed by one each of E, F, G and H etc. If the diamond to be graded appears whiter than the F color stone but not as white as the E, then it is graded as F. In other words, if the diamond's color falls between two grades, it is assigned to the lower grade. Diamond dealers throughout the world have "sample" stones that have been pre-graded and, on being offered a cut diamond, they will match the stone against their own master set and decide what the color of the diamond in question is. This cannot be done with precision if the stone is already set in a mounting. If the diamond is in a yellow-gold mounting, for example, flashes of color from the prongs will seem to make the diamond slightly yellowish and reduce its apparent color grade. Similarly, if a diamond is set in platinum, color distortion will also occur. As prongs can be bent fairly easily by a skilled setter and then bent back to accommodate the stone again, removal of a stone from its mounting presents no safety problem. In the case of important stones, therefore, where a critical judgment is essential, the diamond should always be taken out of the mounting to be graded.

Judging a diamond's color is an art for the connoisseur that takes many years of experience to perfect. Even then, the GIA has found it best to have two or three opinions before a certificate is issued. A D-color diamond is like a piece of ice in a glass of water sitting on a gem dealer's table in Bombay on a bright, sunny day. It has a transparency and whiteness that is incredibly pure, and is so rare that no more than one in a thousand diamonds would possess that quality. White as that is, however, the old Golconda stones were by comparison "whiter than white." Place a Golconda diamond from an old piece of jewelry alongside a modern, recently cut D-color diamond, and the purity of the Golconda stone will become evident. The term "blue-white" refers to the idea that in sunlight, very white stones sometimes fluoresce and thus appear to be blue-white. Because the term was so over-used by zealous salespeople over the last century, it is currently not in favor. Even J, K, L, are merely yellowish, not yellow, and can be considered very beautiful. "Fancy yellow" (or "canary") diamonds are those stones that have a rich yellow, not the off-yellow of J through Z stones. The GIA will label the deeply yellow stones, not by a letter but by a descriptive term such as "fancy" or "intense" or "vivid" yellow (*see next chapter*).

The second parameter of value in diamond grading and connoisseurship is clarity. Here, too, the GIA developed a method of separating flawless stones from imperfect ones. The diamond is inspected with 10X magnification and is examined for internal flaws, fractures, inclusions, carbon spots and so on. If the stone is flawless under 10X magnification, it is so graded on the report. If a diamond has flaws,

depending on how close to the center of the stone the flaws are, and their serious-
ness, it may fall into one of several grades. The descriptions used in grading diamonds are:

> *Flawless.* The complete absence of flaws, whether internal or external, or faults of
> any description when a stone is viewed under 10X binocular magnification.
>
> *Internally flawless.* A complete absence of internal flaws or faults but with minor
> identifying surface characteristics such as growth lines, small naturals or
> extra facets.
>
> *VVS 1–2 (very, very slightly included).* The minute inclusions such as a feather or
> pinpoint that are seen only with difficulty even by the trained eye under
> 10x magnification.
>
> *VS (very slightly included).* Small inclusions that neither affect appearance nor
> durability and cannot be seen with the unaided eye.
>
> *SI (slightly included).* Fairly obvious inclusions under 10X magnification, with the
> lower end of this grade containing stones in which the flaws may be visi-
> ble to the unaided eye when observed through the back of the stone but
> not in a face-up position.
>
> *Imperfect.* Those diamonds in which flaws can be seen with the unaided eye and
> are serious enough to lower the durability of the stone.
>
> See Documentary Illustration p. 237.

Even more than the judging of color, the judging of inclusions requires experience. Just as a D-color stone is exceptionally rare, so too is a flawless diamond:
only one stone in perhaps eight hundred to a thousand falls into this category. The
inclusions of a "VVS" stone can be seen only with difficulty, and a "VS" stone's
inclusions cannot be seen without a jeweler's loupe. It is only when diamonds have
an "SI" or "imperfect" rating that the inclusions block the passage of light in such
a manner that, in fact, optically, the diamond is of less aesthetic interest. It is duller
and less brilliant. These standards having been set up, they are now very much
accepted. Fine retail stores, which traditionally have been the avenue for purchasing important diamonds, generally offer an accompanying gemological certificate
describing a particular stone.

The third parameter of quality is the perfection of cut. If Tolkowski's proportions are used, diamonds will be most brilliant and most dispersive. Proportions,
however, tend to go out the window as the Pythagorean (round numbers)

approach. An unsophisticated purchaser generally will prefer a one-carat diamond to, say, a 0.94-carat stone. With this in mind, the cutter will therefore sacrifice ideal proportions and "swindle the table" or make the pavilion (bottom) of the diamond unnecessarily deep so as to keep the total weight of the stone over a carat. All too often, a larger stone that should be cut to give, say, a 1.75-carat diamond is "swindled" in similar fashion to yield a two-carat size. The ticket on such a stone in the jewelry store may then read "2.01-carat diamond," and the customer will have the pride of knowing that he or she has purchased a two-carat stone. The fact that the stone is slightly less brilliant will not generally be appreciated or understood. The value of diamonds increases disproportionately as the weight increases. Thus, because of its much greater rarity, a two-carat stone is worth more than twice the amount of a one-carat diamond.

A diamond certificate will summarize these quality parameters. In the example shown on p. 237 one can see that the shape and cut of the diamond are mentioned. Ninety per cent of diamonds used in jewelry tend to be cut in the round brilliant fashion, although pear shapes, marquise shapes and emerald cuts are also used often, as dictated by the shape of the rough. A thin, longish diamond rough crystal, for example, generally would be faceted into an emerald cut, since in this instance fashioning the rough into a round shape would result in too great a weight loss. Measurements in millimeters as well as the exact weight of the stone are given; the proportions and finish are stated, together with the all-important clarity grade and color grade.

With the advent of computers and the wide dissemination of gem certification reports, very complex price grades have been established for diamonds of different qualities and weights. These grades will tell you, for example, what a D flawless diamond or a D–VVSI, one-carat stone should cost. Computer records can be used to tell you the price "history" of various categories, such as the price of a D-color, VSI stone two-and-a-half years ago as compared with today. It should always be kept in mind that the number of D-flawless diamonds is minute. J. F. Moyersoen, for example, estimates the total output at no more than 3,000–4,000 carats per year (or about 1,000–2,000 individual stones).

Finally, unlike the case with rubies, sapphires and emeralds, where certification is not as widely accepted as in the diamond trade, the certificate itself has an international acceptance. A diamond dealer in New York might telephone his counterpart in Hong Kong and offer a stone of E color, VVSI clarity, in a round brilliant cut, 1.24 carats, for $6,000 per carat, as part of a large wholesale "series," and from this description the Hong Kong merchant will be able to visualize almost precisely the diamond being offered. The GIA has set up, in effect, an "Esperanto" language of diamonds, usable by all gemologists and dealers throughout the world. At first blush, it would seem to be an unquestionably good thing for the diamond trade that such a means of communication has been devised, yet people are starting to attribute paramount importance to the certificate, instead of looking at the diamond to which it applies. Hand some people a diamond and a certificate and they will study the certificate, but the true connoisseur will, of course, look carefully at the diamond first.

The future of the diamond trade is very much in the hands of De Beers Consolidated Mines. Since the late nineteenth century De Beers has been a remarkable stabilizing force in the diamond world. Diamonds, it must be remembered, have a backward sloping demand curve: if people believe that prices will go up, they tend to buy diamonds. The prospect of a "close-out sale" would cause a great loss of faith in the diamond as an investment, and therefore the whole production and marketing philosophy of De Beers has been geared toward stabilizing prices over a long period. To understand De Beers and the diamond world, one must examine that company's beginnings.

Like the Indian diamonds, the first South African diamonds discovered in the 1880s were of river origin. Small concentrations around the Orange River were found, and soon a full-fledged diamond rush was under way. Two brothers, D. A. and J.N. De Beer, sober Boer farmers, found diamond crystals on their land and subsequently sold their property to miners at a very high price. Diamond fever spread throughout South Africa, with large numbers of prospectors coming to the area from all over the world. Outcroppings of yellowish and bluish-green mineral deposits near the town of Kimberley were found, and these came to be called "kimberlite." The Kimberley mine turned out to have the richest diamond deposits ever discovered. The competition to obtain diamonds resembled the Gold Rush of another day. Within a few feet of each other, individual miners had staked out their claim and begun digging. Gradually, the land around Kimberley was dug in such a helter-skelter fashion, with so many interconnecting tunnels, that large-scale cave-ins began to occur.

Two of the main characters who emerged at that time were Cecil Rhodes, known to the world as the creator of De Beers Consolidated Mines Ltd, and Barney Barnato, a fabulous though less well-known personality. From the East End of London, Barnato went to South Africa with his brother in the hopes of making his fortune as a song-and-dance man, comedian, boxer, and all-round entertainer. He traded in beautiful ostrich feathers, sugar and spices, but, as everybody knew in the 1880s, the true wealth of South Africa lay in its newly discovered diamond areas. With the money he made as a trader, Barnato began to accumulate large holdings in different sections of the Kimberley mining area. Eventually, he formed his own very profitable mining and trading company.

Cecil Rhodes, a year older than Barnato, was an Oxford-educated classicist and of a quite different disposition and character. Where Barnato was gregarious, easy going and shrewd, Rhodes was taciturn and careful. Though an adventurer, eager to create an empire, Rhodes also went to South Africa for the sake of his health. He soon became involved in mining at the Kimberley diamond fields. It did not take him long to see the necessity of uniting the diamond mines into a co-operative cartel, in order to eliminate the reigning chaos, ballooning production and unsafe working conditions. Rhodes suggested to Barnato that they consolidate into one large company under the De Beers corporate banner, so that the new organization could market all the Kimberley diamonds. Barnato also saw the advantages of centralized diamond selling, but he believed that Rhodes should sell out to him and that he, as the better trader, should be the dominant figure in the Kimberley area. After several years of conflict, the two men came to an agreement: Barnato became a life-time governor, and Rhodes the chairman, of the newly formed De Beers Consolidated Mines Ltd, which then proceeded to buy up other diamond fields and also established a very strong position in the gold mining areas of South Africa. In 1899 De Beers controlled at least ninety per cent of the world's diamond production.

In the early 1900s another man who would figure prominently in De Beers' history, Sir Ernest Oppenheimer, went to South Africa as a broker for a London diamond firm. He achieved great importance by acquiring huge diamond mine holdings in southwestern Africa. These were merged into De Beers, and Sir Ernest subsequently became the head of the company. During the Depression years Oppenheimer was exceptionally courageous and forceful. He curtailed production completely in most mines, sopping up available supply and stabilizing diamond prices. As a result of his efforts, diamond prices fell during the Depression by only approximately fifty per cent. This drop compares favorably with the catastrophic decline of stock markets throughout the world in the same period. Price stabilization during those troublesome times led to the immense post-war confidence placed in diamonds as a store of value. After World War II, De Beers was able to introduce diamonds in a significant way to Japan and other Far Eastern countries.

The diamond engagement ring as well as the important "solitaire" diamond ring are now in demand throughout the world by both men and women, and, with its firm hold on the market supply, De Beers accounts for over eighty per cent of the sales of uncut diamonds throughout the world.

In the early 1970s De Beers sent an exploration team into Botswana. During the first twelve years of searching, they found only a handful of diamonds and pyrope garnet crystals, indicating the presence of a diamond pipe. On such results few major corporations would have continued the search. Finally, however, near Orapa, a water station in western Botswana, the second largest diamond pipe in the world was found. Major finds have also been made in Siberia, elsewhere in Botswana, in Lesotho and in South America. It is a mark of De Beers' far-sightedness and "liberality" that the corporation chose to offer to Botswana a partnership in De Beers itself in exchange for the enormous amounts of diamonds that were found in Botswana. Botswana has become, as a government, a shareholder in De Beers itself, which has led to Botswana's citizens having one of the highest per capita incomes in Africa—albeit recognizing that per capita incomes in Africa as a continent have remained abysmally low. The principle, however, of De Beers becoming a partner with a sovereign state, I think, will be a hallmark of the future in the world of diamonds.

In the 1990s, major finds continued to be made in the former Soviet Union. As one can well imagine, the Russian government was under enormous pressure to try to maximize their income from these finds. On the one hand, De Beers was a steady and active buyer; on the other, Soviets continue to have a feeling that in boom times in the diamond trade they were not maximizing their income. The share of De Beers in the 1990s dropped to approximately 65% of total world production.

In the 1990s also, many individual diamond mines were opened in Canada. Various combinations of wildcatting discoveries as well as experienced large multinational mining companies, such as Rio Tinto, entered the Canadian diamond market as mining operations and marketing companies. A fascinating blend was the commitment by Tiffany, a major purchaser of fine diamonds, to enter into an agreement to purchase diamonds, not through the De Beers cartel, but rather directly through a Canadian diamond exploration company.

Under the leadership of the son of Harry Oppenheimer, Nicholas, diamonds have become an immense business. In recent years, De Beers has entered into a marketing arrangement with Louis Vuitton Moët Hennessey (LVMH), and the two have opened several stores in diamond capitals of the world.

De Beers has always been a family dominated corporation, and the

Oppenheimer family, along with other corporate entities, has bought back shares of De Beers and turned it into a private company. Brand names for diamonds have become the order of the day. The innate worldwide attraction to diamonds will now be given a further "sophisticated" merchandising effort.

De Beers has perfected and employs a system of certificates to insure that from the mine to the end consumer of a finished piece of jewelry no diamonds from "conflict aeas" are bought or sold. Behind all these sales figures is the diamond itself. Spectacular diamonds can be seen in Iran, where a collection from the Golconda mines sits on trays much like chocolates displayed in a sweet shop. There are over thirty diamonds of at least 50 carats each in one Iranian museum. In the Smithsonian Institution one can see the Portuguese Diamond, 127 carats, as well as a magnificent rough diamond crystal. The Tower of London houses the Crown Jewels, including the Cullinan Diamond (the "Great Star of Africa") the largest cut diamond in the world, 530 carats, mounted in the Sovereign's Sceptre; its little sister, a mere 317 carats, the Cullinan II, is set in the Imperial State Crown. In the Louvre in Paris one can see the Regent Diamond, found in India in 1701 and carried, via brigands, shipwrecked sea captains and the English aristocracy to the Duc d'Orléans, Prince Regent of France, in 1717. And, of course, in all the auction houses and the fine retail jewelers' windows, one can see displayed, at any time of the year, the dispersive and brilliant beauty of diamonds.

What is the future for the aesthetics and acceptance of diamond? For two thousand years in all cultures, the diamond has had a powerful allure. In India the social structure was formerly ordered according to diamond aesthetics. In ancient Rome leading figures were awarded diamonds (although not of gem quality) by the emperor. Renaissance princes kept whole ateliers fashioning diamonds. Modern-day tycoons purchase diamonds, setting up a standard of "emulation" in the imagination of all segments of society. Today, however, with an increasing accent on diamonds as an investment, as opposed to diamonds displayed in a jewel as a work of art, we are faced with the danger that the diamond may become a demystified object. In my opinion, however, diamonds will retain their mystery, even after they have been dissected and described with the aid of microscopes, spectroscopes, computers and certificates.

In the Talmud it is written, "To understand the invisible world one must carefully study the visible." Diamonds will always be a magical window facing the invisible world.

FIVE

COLORED DIAMOND

"God never repeats himself."
—Rabbi Nachman of Bratzlav

THE RAREST COLORED diamonds—red, blue and green—might at first
sight seem to duplicate respectively the ruby, the sapphire and the emerald,
but close examination reveals that they are quite different from other colored gemstones. Just as among other colored gemstones, pride of place
(and of value) is accorded to the ruby, so, too, among diamonds is it accorded to
the red stones, followed by the green and then the blue varieties.

An intense red diamond, like a ten-carat, pigeon-blood Burma ruby, is virtually unobtainable. Stories told about a truly red diamond always prove to be
secondhand. A .95-carat red was auctioned, a five carat red has been seen. Such
stones are exceedingly rare. A deep-green diamond is also found only rarely. The
best-known blue diamond, the Hope Diamond, is often described as being "sapphire blue," but in fact it is a "Ceylon sapphire blue" (see chapter 2). Visitors to the
Smithsonian in Washington are struck by how much of an inky overtone is present in the Hope, giving it a steel-like blue color. Occasionally, one will encounter
a diamond of medium-blue intensity, comparable to a Burma sapphire. The 35.32-
carat Wittelsbach Diamond, which was owned in 1722 by the Austrian Hapsburgs,
is such a stone. After being sold in 1932, it resurfaced briefly on the Antwerp
wholesale market thirty years later, only to be photographed and later resold to a
private collector. Aaron Gutwirth's description of it (he was a member of the

Komkommer group that purchased it in 1962) characterized the shade of the stone as "blue with a hint of purple but not with the same degree of gray-green of the Hope Diamond."

In gem quality all colored diamonds are rare indeed. Perhaps one in a hundred thousand diamonds has a deep enough natural color to qualify as a "fine, fancy colored diamond." Why are fancy colored diamonds so rare? Gemologically, what gives white diamonds a yellow color is the admixture of nitrogen, minute amounts of which will give rise to a yellowish stone, becoming increasingly yellow with any increase in the amount of nitrogen present. Blue diamonds are the result of an admixture of boron. An odd feature of blue diamonds is that, unlike other diamonds, they are part of the "II-B" family and are semi-conductors of electricity. Almost all of the semi-conducting diamonds found today come from the Premier Mine in South Africa, but the Kollur blues from Golconda, India, also conducted electricity; the blue Hope Diamond, in fact, exhibits these same conductive characteristics. The color in very light-green diamonds would seem to result from minute traces of radioactivity, and the color in brown diamonds—like the yellows—from an addition of nitrogen.

With the exception of yellow and brown diamonds, which are occasionally found among rough stones mined in South Africa, the vast majority of reds, blues, and greens originated in the fabled historic mines of India. In his account of his travels, Tavernier, the seventeenth-century gem merchant, described the tricks of the trade in India and, most importantly, he described and drew (see p. 236) fabulous diamonds that he saw; indeed, because one of his customers was Louis XIV, virtually all important stones came his way. Thus, Tavernier could describe how he had seen a fine 112-carat blue diamond in the Kollur mine in Golconda in 1661. Herbert Tillander, after some complicated gymnastics, has traced that stone's history leading up to its re-cutting into the Hope Diamond that Harry Winston finally donated to the Smithsonian 286 years later.

Similarly, in the fabulous former royal collection of both colored and white diamonds and colored stones in Iran, there is a magnificent gem, considered by many to be the finest pink diamond in the world, called the Sea of Light, or Darya-i-Nur. It is a flat tablet in a rectangular form, weighing 182 carats. One can look straight through the center of the stone. The only brilliance is on the rectangle's edges, where there are step-cut facets. At first, it is difficult to detect the pink, but after a period of looking, hints of pink start to emerge slowly from the stone. These lifelike nuances of color increase as one moves one's head back and

94

forth. The stone is mesmerizing because of these delicate flashes of color. In 1834 the Sultan, Fath Ali Shah, could not resist having his name inscribed in Persian on one of the pavilion facets of the stone. This pink gem is therefore the most alluring graffiti-bearing object known today. The history of this stone, too, has been worked back to Tavernier's original purchasing tours in the seventeenth century. The Darya-i-Nur, together with another stone weighing 60 carats, the Nurul-'Ain (Light of the Eye), originally formed the Great Table diamond seen by Tavernier. In the 1830s the Great Table was recut, yielding these two specimen stones. Jones Brydges was able to trace the history of the Great Table diamond by observing that both the shade of pink and the translucency of the two diamonds are identical. Allowing for inevitable wastage in cutting, the combined weight of the two smaller stones corresponds to the Great Table's original weight, 250 carats. Tavernier wrote:

> Being at Golconda, I saw this stone, and it was the biggest I ever saw in my life in a merchant's hands. It was valued at 500,000 rupees, or 750,000 livres of our money. I offered 400,000 rupees but could not have it.

In his book, Tavernier was anxious to show that he not only saw the finest stones but also that he was a judicious buyer—and even Louis XIV loved a bargain. The stone he described eventually found its way to Delhi. In 1739, in the sack of that city, Nadir Shah took the stone, along with the rest of the Mughal treasure, to Persia. These treasures are now in the former royal jewel collections of Iran.

Indians, however, preferred the purely colorless, white stones to colored diamonds, perhaps because the diamond colors did not truly match the pure hues of ruby, sapphire and emerald. Tavernier wrote:

> All orientals are of our opinion in the matter of whiteness, and I have always remarked that they love the whitest pearls, the most limpid diamonds, the whitest bread and the whitest women.

As a result, some of the truly fine-colored diamonds did find their way to the West. However, the Indian mines were virtually exhausted by the end of the eighteenth century, and the Brazilian diamond deposits discovered in the late eighteenth century did not add much to the supply of fancy colored diamonds. South Africa, of course, has a tremendous output of diamonds, but the number of colored stones produced is quite small. Yellow diamonds and orange diamonds, though, are found in small numbers in Kimberley and in the Premier Mine, while Bultfontein produces light-purple stones. De Beers Consolidated Mines Ltd has a collection showing the magnificent range of shades occurring naturally in colored diamonds. De Beers, by having stabilized the market for decades, and by carefully selecting the proper cutters, is still able to ensure that the prices of colored diamonds have not become completely prohibitive.

Yellow diamonds fit into many categories, depending upon the strength of the yellow. If there is just a trace of yellow, the color is considered off-white, with the hint of yellow being "neither here nor there" and not adding to the diamond's beauty (*see* chapter 4). The Gemological Institute of America has graded white and faintly yellow stones on a scale from "D" to "Z," but once the yellow becomes more pronounced than that of a 2-color stone, a diamond is described as being "natural color yellow."

It often takes many years' experience of comparing shades of yellow in diamonds to develop a connoisseurship in judgment. In the same way that a dealer in colored stones judges gemstones, the essential method a diamond merchant uses is to lay a yellow diamond alongside others. Normally, expert advice is required when deciding on a substantial purchase of colored diamonds; leading jewelry stores have traditionally provided such guidance for their customers. By constantly comparing yellow diamonds, one's eye adapts to the different shades: these can be lemon yellow, pure yellow, brownish yellow (often termed "champagne") and orange yellow (termed "jonquil").

A natural yellow diamond having a light-yellow shade will be certified by the GIA as a "fancy light-yellow natural color diamond." If the yellow is a bit deeper, the certificate will read "fancy yellow natural color diamond." If the color is a gem yellow, that is a rich, deep, saturated yellow, the diamond will be termed "fancy intense yellow," but such stones are very rare. The highest accolade for a yellow diamond is one that has an extraordinarily saturated color and is termed by the GIA as "Vivid."

A fabulous example of a yellow diamond may be seen in New York at the Tiffany & Co. store on Fifth Avenue. Downstairs, in a showcase discreetly placed in a corner of the main floor, is the magnificent 128-carat cushion-shaped stone, known as the Tiffany Diamond, the finest canary diamond in the world, "canary" being the connoisseur's term for yellow without any admixture of green or orange. The Tiffany Diamond, mined in South Africa in 1878, is so mesmerizing that after it had been cut its facets were miscounted. It was not until 1945 that the discovery was made that there are in fact 90 facets on the stone, not 101 as had been believed.

104 One of earliest known colored diamond rings. The amber colored diamond was set in the medieval gold ring, c. 14th century.

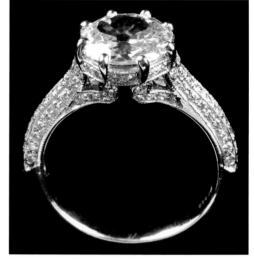

105 *A pair of earrings, one containing a fancy light-pink diamond, the other a fancy blue stone, both pear-shaped and of natural color.*

106 (RIGHT) *A very fine orange-pink Golconda diamond mined and cut in India, c. 1680. The shade of color reminiscent of the delicate pink in the Darya-i-Nur diamond in the Bank Melli (a museum in Teheran) which houses the greatest surviving collection of Mughal Indian jewelry.*

107 (BELOW) *A bar pin that contains an emerald-cut fancy blue diamond, a round white diamond and a hexagonal pink diamond. Although the stones are cut differently, the tonality and brilliance are so well matched that the resulting piece is a magnificent ensemble.*

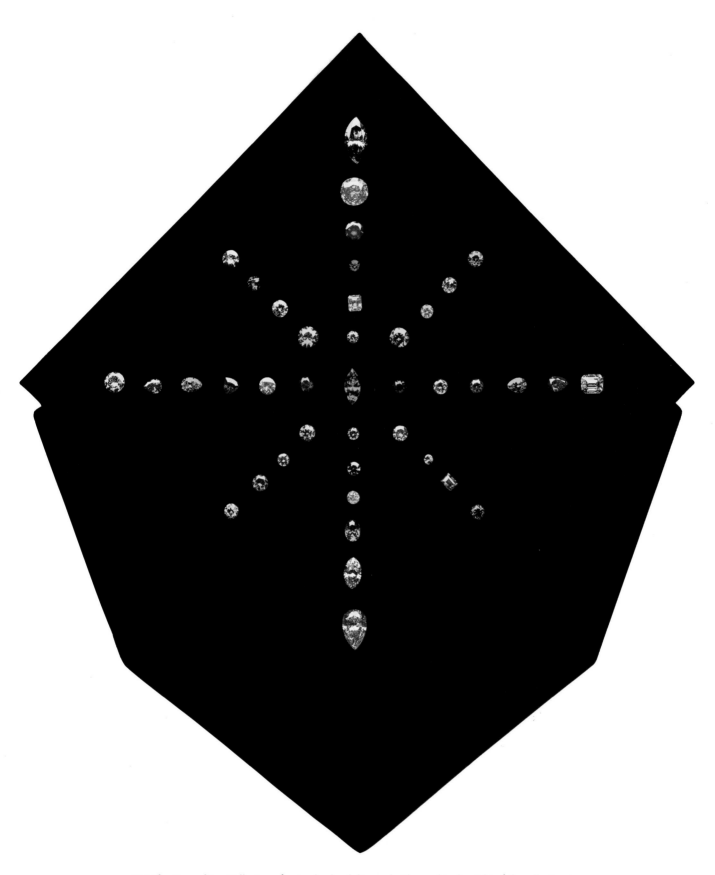

108 The Gumuchian Collection of natural colored diamonds. The combined weight of the collection is 63.87 carats. When on display at the American Museum of Natural History, it was considered to be one of the finest collections of colored diamonds.

109, 110 The green transmitter is a rare and spectacular type of green diamond. This 2 carat cushion-cut Brazilian diamond is intense greenish yellow in daylight (and fluorescent light) and yellowish brown in incandescent light. It was given by Emperor Pedro II (1825-91) of Brazil to his niece. Connoisseurs call this shade of diamond color chartreuse.

111 *A jonquil diamond that is yellowish with strong orange overtones.*

112 *A Tiffany ring, c. 1910, containing a rare natural blue Golconda diamond with a well-matcthed fancy yellow diamond.*

113 (ABOVE) The Tiffany Diamond. The color of this magnificent 128.51-carat cushion-shaped yellow diamond is free from brown or green. The stone, which is cushion cut, has 90 facets and exhibits extraordinary brilliance.

114 An early 18th century very fine Indian flat portrait diamond set in an Edwardian setting. Typically, these diamonds were bought by maharajas in the early 1900's to be reset in "very stylish" platinum jewelry.

115 *A table-cut olive-green diamond seen side-by-side with a round chartreuse (yellow and green) diamond.*

116 Ranges of color in pink diamonds. LEFT, *a fancy intense pink oval;* CENTER, *a fancy light pink;* RIGHT, *a smaller fancy pink pear-shaped stone.*

117 *A trio of colored diamonds.* LEFT: *A golconda faint pink diamond set by Chaumet in a ring, Paris, 1915;* CENTER: *A rare natural blue-green diamond cut and mined in India, 1700;* RIGHT: *A yellow and greenish-yellow diamond set in Edwardian England, c. 1910.*

118 *A 3.21-carat fancy blue diamond; although the blue is not intense, it is of a pure character.*

119 Irradiated diamonds. Although irradiated diamonds sell for a fraction of the price commanded by their "natural" counterparts, they can still be extremely decorative, and have an important place in the commercial jewelry world.

The mistake is understandable, for the eye is easily confused by the extreme brilliance and the color of this stone. At one point in the 1960s, an enthusiastic neophyte salesperson at Tiffany asked Walter Hoving, the president of Tiffany, what would happen if he were able to sell the Tiffany diamond. Hoving replied laconically, "I'd fire you."

Brown diamonds are more common than yellow, and to make such stones rather more appealing, diamond merchants will describe the different shades in gastronomical terms. The most prized diamonds in the brown family are the "coffee" browns, with only a hint of black in them. A still more intense shade is termed "chocolate" brown. If the brown is deep but has a touch of yellow, the stone will be called a "cognac" diamond (cognac is a deeper, more intense brown than champagne yellow-brown).

Green diamonds are sometimes compared to emeralds, but even the largest known example, the 41-carat Dresden Green, is apple-green—more yellow than green. Occasionally, one may see a light green-yellow, but this color is not as sought after as the pure-yellow or pure-green stones. If the green is a bit saturated, it would be called, by a good friend of mine, a "chartreuse," having a mixture of green, yellow and a hint of orange and gray. Finally, a darkish, metallic-looking olive green is also sometimes seen. As a general rule the purer the green, the more in demand will be the diamond.

Mauve and violet-colored stones also appear on the market from time to time. In a setting of gold or platinum, these delicate shades are often enhanced substantially. For such stones the GIA has appropriate color rubrics such as "light violet natural color diamond."

Pink diamonds are especially rare, though not as difficult to obtain as the reds or pure greens. A magnificent seven-carat pink, cut in a round shape, was sold at auction in Geneva in 1980. In this stone, the pink was a delicate light shade, not as fugitive as the Darya-i-Nur but still of captivating quality, and the diamond sold for $123,000 per carat. In 1999 in New York Sotheby sold a 14 carat fancy intense pink diamond for $2,000,000. In 2002, in Geneva, a pear shape three-carat blue diamond fetched $150,000 per carat; its color was more steel-blue, but because of the great rarity of blue diamonds, even a stone termed by the GIA as "light blue," which sometimes seems so metallic, is much sought-after today. The description "faint" is used in the case of the least saturated shades of pink and blue. Progressive additional amounts of blue will cause diamonds to be graded "very light blue," "fancy light blue" or "fancy vivid blue."

Black diamonds have the lowest value among colored diamonds. As printers know, there are in practice countless shades of black. Occasionally, one will find a black stone (generally rescued from the industrial boxes of De Beers diamonds) that has a touch of green in it and is highly reflective. In Amsterdam there is a 44-carat, pear-shaped stone that is considered gem black. In Sumatra and in other parts of the East, black diamonds are worn as mourning stones. This practice spread to Portugal, where one sometimes sees a black diamond ring being worn and treasured as a family heirloom.

Sometimes a colored diamond is not what it appears to be. Some years ago Robert Crowningshield, director of the GIA laboratory in New York, was testing a magnificent yellow diamond. The spectral lines and other properties of the stone intrigued him, and he sent it to Dr. Eduard Gübelin in Lucerne for further examination. When the stone arrived with its preliminary GIA certification, Dr. Gübelin saw it in daylight and immediately telephoned New York. "You sent me a green diamond instead of a yellow diamond," he exclaimed. As it happens, there are, occasionally, yellow diamonds that turn green when exposed to ultraviolet light, which is present in sunlight. If the diamond is heated (or irradiated) or kept out of the sun, it will slowly revert to its original color. Such stones are called "chameleon" diamonds. The mystery of why this occurs was finally understood in 2001 and described in *A Green Diamond*. An overabundance of oxygen in the diamond's lattice structure leads to one of the most startling color changes in the world of gems. An entirely different form of color change—from yellow to intense greenish yellow—occurs in the Dom Pedro Diamond once owned by the emperor of Brazil. There absorption of ultra violet light in daylight accounts for the rare color change.

All of the stones described above are the "aristocrats" of the colored diamond world, but what about the "pretenders to the throne"—the artificially colored diamonds? As early as 1904 experiments were conducted to alter the color of natural diamond. Basically, the method used was to subject the diamonds to radioactive treatment (irradiation). It was the brilliant British scientist, Sir William Crookes, who first treated diamonds with radium, and this resulted in a color change from off-white to a tourmaline-green shade. One such stone, presently in the British Museum, has kept its depth of color since treatment by Crookes at the beginning of the century. Radium, however, is far too expensive and because of its radioactive nature, far too dangerous, to be used commercially.

Today's methods often employ a cyclotron. The diamond is bombarded by a stream of high-energy particles which pass through the entire diamond. As a result, some of the atoms in the lattice-work structure of the diamond are rearranged. If even one atom is knocked from the lattice structure, the entire absorption pattern of the stone will be altered. Dr. F. A. Raal, manager of De Beers Diamond Research Laboratory in Johannesburg, has pointed out that the artificial coloring process is "additive," or in practical terms, "a bad diamond cannot be made good." Thus, a slightly yellowish (off-white) stone cannot be made into a fine white stone, but white or off-white diamonds can indeed be turned into yellows or into other colors. Brown diamonds are the raw material used to produce irradiated blues.

There has been a lot of technological development in this field, resulting from enormous demand combined with the extreme scarcity of natural colored diamonds. A one-carat, top-color blue stone can fetch over $100,000 if it is both gem and natural, whereas a similar, one-carat, irradiated diamond would command only upwards of $3,000. A one-carat light apple-green diamond can be worth $120,000 in its naturally colored state, whereas in the irradiated state a similar stone can command only $2,500. The cost of the original material for irradiated diamonds is kept down by the use of off-white stones. Generally, the diamonds that the GIA grades either "M" or "N" color, or lower in the scale, are used in the irradiation process. Because of a peculiar geological phenomenon, the white diamonds chosen for irradiation must be non-fluorescent, for diamonds that fluoresce after irradiation reveal a mixture of colors and often have a muddy look, and are therefore assiduously avoided.

Just as in heat-treating or "cooking" sapphires and rubies, there are different "recipes" for altering the color of diamonds in this way. The secrets of the methods used are jealously guarded by the merchants who artificially color diamonds. It is understood, however, that success will depend upon the choice of the original material to be treated. Certain shades of yellowish diamond will normally yield shades of pink, blue, green, yellow or orange. Also, diamonds with certain piqués (imperfections) will sometimes shatter in the enhancement process.

How do artificially colored diamonds differ from naturally colored diamonds? In a natural yellow diamond, if the yellow is intense, it will be slightly less "metallic" looking than an irradiated yellow diamond. In the light-yellow range, irradiated stones will tend to have an orange overcast, as opposed to the more general lemon-yellow shade of the natural light yellows. In a green diamond, the natural green will be very light, whereas the artificial green will be a deeper shade. The natural blues vary from steel blue—less prized, of course—to the light purple, light cornflower and, very occasionally, medium-intensity pure blue. Irradiated stones often achieve a very intense blue, extremely brilliant, but often with a steel-like overcast and a slight touch of green. In the case of the browns, irradiated stones tend to be more of a brandy shade and are often more intense in their brilliance than their natural counterparts. It takes a connoisseur's eye to separate the shades that distinguish naturally colored from artificially colored diamonds.

Any major colored diamond of gem quality sold in a fine retail store will always be accompanied today by a certificate from a gemological laboratory, stating that the color is natural. The GIA uses a spectroscope to separate natural diamonds from their irradiated counterparts. Natural-color diamond has characteristic spectral bands, but this feature will be altered in a diamond that has been treated artificially.

Fine colored diamonds offered for sale today are rarely newly mined stones. When such stones are found and distributed skillfully through De Beers, they pose a terrific challenge to the rough cutter. Recently, a diamond sight-box was given out containing a three-carat cleavage that yielded a magnificent pink, but colored diamonds tend to occur, according to Dr. Raal, in more poorly shaped rough. The well-formed octahedral crystals often characteristic of colorless white diamonds are not typical of colored diamonds. The "impurities" such as nitrogen "deform" the diamond crystals, with the result that most colored diamonds are found in nature in the random cleavage pattern, and these pieces of rough are difficult to cut. Rough that will yield colored diamonds is, in the vast majority of cases, classified immediately by De Beers as "specials." These are sold on a one-by-one basis to highly skilled New York and Antwerp diamond cutters, who know how best to fashion the most beautiful cut stone from the rough crystal. Only very occasionally will a colored diamond be cut in Israel or in India. In those countries the more commercial, smaller, white diamonds are generally cut.

Cutting pink diamonds is occasionally hazardous, for the color is often partially hidden under a coating. Also, pinks have sometimes evaporated under the heat of the cutting wheel, and cutters are especially careful when putting a colored diamond on the wheel. Similarly, in blue diamonds and yellows, the color is often not uniformly spread throughout the crystal. The cutter's skill lies in making sure that the most intense shade of color is reflected through the table of the diamond. Color in blues and yellows often runs in parallel lines. After the diamond has been cut, this color banding can usually be seen with a loupe, if the stone is tilted and viewed at an angle.

The vast majority of colored diamonds appearing on the market today are from estate and secondhand jewelry pieces. In both Europe and America one can often see Art Deco or Art Nouveau jewelry and pieces dating from the 1930s made in fabulous forms of vases, flowers and other whimsical designs. The mixture of colored diamonds, with both their brilliance and shades of color, presents a world of living "flora" and "fauna." All too often, unfortunately, such elaborate pieces will be taken apart. The small, naturally colored melee diamonds may be used as a border for the creation of a modern ring, and often the more substantial half-carat, one-carat and larger stones will be recut and mounted as solitaires or in twin rings. There are some important diamond jewelry collections—not worn but displayed—colored in private ownership today.

In order to gain an appreciation of the fineness of colored diamonds, museum visits can be very rewarding. Pride of place would go to the Aurora Collection once displayed at the American Museum of Natural History in New York. There, one may see a collection of colored diamonds of every known shade. The museum also had on display a fine 65.60-carat brown diamond, the Golden Maharaja, remarkable for its color brilliance. For a time, in 1981, an outstanding grouping, the Rainbow collection of colored diamonds, was on display there. In that collection a "brick-red" diamond was especially appreciated by fanciers of colored diamonds. The Smithsonian, of course, also proudly displays the fabulous Hope Diamond.

The collection in Tehran has, in addition to the Darya-i-Nur and the Nur-ul-'Ain, a series of old European-cut, cushion-shaped, pink and lavender diamonds of fifteen carats and above. Some of these pinks (and blue and yellow diamonds) were fashioned into tiaras and crowns. Aside from these old Indian stones, there are several dozen South African yellows that were cut from enormous diamonds in the late nineteenth century. In the Golestan Palace in Iran, Naisir ud-Din Shah was so enamored of precious stones that he set up a cutting factory to fashion gems within his palace; many of these stones weigh over 100 carats apiece. In Istanbul there is a fabulous 86-carat violet diamond in a ring in the Topkapi Museum, along with many pieces of Mughal jewelry containing pinks and blues. In the Soviet Union there is a historic tablet-shaped yellow diamond of 88 carats, of Golconda origin—a gift to the Russian people after the assassination of their ambassador in Persia in 1829. The 41-carat Dresden Green is on display in the Green Vault in Dresden. Visiting these museums will be like viewing a retrospective showing of the riches of Golconda, and the Mughal courts of the sixteenth century.

John Mandeville, a traveler to the East in the fourteenth century, wrote that diamonds take "pleasure in assuming in turns the colors proper to other gems." This is not quite true, for in reality colored diamonds present nuances of red, blue, green, yellow and brown not found in other gems. Given the extraordinary brilliance and the inherent color of natural diamonds, it can still be asserted that "God never repeats himself."

SIX

PEARL

"I owe my fine health and long life to the two pearls I have swallowed every morning of my life since I was twenty."

—K. MIKIMOTO at the age of ninety-four

N THE EARLY twentieth century in India, visitors to the palace of the Gaekwar of Baroda were treated, if they were fortunate, to the sight of the most beautiful pearl-covered object in the world: a sumptuous carpet measuring 10 ft x 6 ft (305 x 183 cm), with its entire area filled with natural oriental pearls. Each pearl in the carpet had been drilled and threaded, and along one end of the rug, discreetly sewn in, were carefully fashioned diamonds. The Indian light, with its great intensity, played luxuriously on the carpet's surface, causing the masses of pearls to shimmer before the Gaekwar's throne. The blending of the pearls was done in such a way that waves of color—nuances of white—seemed to sweep across the surface. Each pearl seemed perfectly matched, whereas, in fact, the pearls had all been skillfully graded and combined to produce a gentle shading off, to silvery- or creamy-white, from the center toward the outside perimeters of the carpet.

Different accounts of the reason for the creation of this carpet exist. A late nineteenth-century writer said that it had been created, a generation earlier, out of the pearl treasury by the previous Gaekwar; the pearl carpet was a handy way to "store" all of the Baroda pearls which, in a loose state, were difficult to keep track of. Another, more novel, reason offered was that his son, who succeeded to the title of Gaekwar, himself created the piece as a sumptuous gift for an Englishwoman with whom he had fallen in love. The sober-minded English resident "advisor" of the day then told the Gaekwar politely but firmly that the province of Baroda

111

could not afford to part with such a costly treasure and, in fact, the pearl carpet remained in Baroda.

Natural pearl is one of the glories of nature. Unlike diamonds or colored stones, pearl is found in its completed natural state. Apart from being drilled, it does not need to be recut or fashioned by the hand of man. The tradition of diving in search of pearls has lasted for over two thousand years. A description by Tavernier closely matches twentieth-century accounts:

> I am aware that according to the testimony of some ancient authors who were not well instructed in these matters, it was commonly believed that pearl originates from the dew of heaven and that but one is found in each oyster. But experience proves the contrary, for as regards the first, the oyster does not stir from the bottom of the sea where the dew cannot penetrate, and sometimes it is necessary to dive for them to a depth of twelve cubits [about 20 ft]. . . . It is common to find as many as six or seven pearls in a single oyster.

Tavernier's observations, based as they were on first-hand viewing of the Bahrain fisheries, were accurate. Essentially, a natural pearl results from the presence of an irritant in an oyster. The irritant may be in the form of a grain of sand or a living thing such as an insect or other foreign body. When the irritant enters the shell of the mollusk, it becomes trapped by the soft tissue, the mantle, and the irritated mantle secretes a material that surrounds the irritant. The latter becomes the "nucleus" of a future pearl, and many further shell-like layers of conchiolin and aragonite are created over a period of years. If the original irritant affixes itself to the inner shell surface, a blister pearl results. If the irritant is animate, the pearl is formed toward the center of the mantle. The pearl's size is influenced by the size and shape of the host oyster, and by the pearl's place within it: the larger the host shell, the larger the possible pearl size.

In Bahrain in the early nineteenth century, eight thousand boats containing at least thirty thousand Arab male pearl divers would set out each morning to dive for pearls. The diving day would begin at five o'clock. First, the divers would turn toward Mecca and intone the morning prayers. After a light breakfast the diving would begin. (Experienced divers were able to stay under water for over 110 seconds.) Each diver would descend with a knife in his mouth and slash away at an oyster, once sighted. Often, relatives would be on the boat, ready to open the oyster as soon as it was found. The divers' work was rarely rewarded with success, for although millions of oysters would be fished, only very few would yield pearls. If a great pearl with a diameter of over 6 mm were found, it would be offered first to the local ruler, but otherwise Hindu traders would buy any pearls found, dealing directly with the divers. Profits for the divers were generally small, but the possibility of acquiring tremendous sudden riches fuelled their incredible, patient efforts. In his book *The Pearl*, Frederick Kunz describes how, once purchased by the dealers, the pearls would be sent to Bombay for cleaning and drilling. There, a solution of peroxide and other "mystery" ingredients was used first to clean the pearls. The whiter pearls resulting would then be sorted and drilled. One of the reasons why pearls were shipped immediately to Bombay was that a ready market awaited them there. As with diamonds, and emeralds, Indian maharajas and maharanis were great connoisseurs of gem pearls and would be offered the finest from which to choose. (Western pearl merchants who traveled to Bombay would get only the second-best pearls.) Having ready customers at hand over the centuries enabled the Indian pearl merchants to pay the highest prices in the world for pearls. The pearl collection of the Nizam of Hyderabad, as well as the collections of the former rulers of Patiala and Dholpur were as extraordinary as the Baroda ensemble. In fact, the Rana of Dholpur was known as the "Prince of Pearls" because of his habit, when greeting foreign guests, of wearing twelve matched strands of pearls, each with a 12-mm diameter, as well as one choker of jumbo-sized pearls and a modest little cap, also intertwined with pearls.

The Persian Gulf was not the only source for pearls. Elsewhere, between Ceylon and India, Tamil divers would search for pearl oysters. The numbers found there were, however, only a quarter of the Persian Gulf catch and the pearls tended to be a creamier, less white, color; also, Ceylonese pearls were less lustrous. However, both these and Persian Gulf pearls were fine enough to be called "oriental." Other sources of natural pearl were Venezuela and, in the United States, Mississippi, for freshwater pearls. Almost all freshwater pearls are of larger size than the pearls of the Persian Gulf and Ceylon, but lack the shimmering orient of the Asian pearls. In practice, Persian Gulf pearls have always been far and away the most desired and highly priced.

The standards for judging pearls have remained constant throughout history. What was valued in Talmudic times and in ancient Rome has similarly been sought after in Byzantium, in Renaissance Venice and in twentieth-century Paris. Pearl dealers first look to shape. A pearl may be round, button-shaped, pear-shaped or irregular (known as "baroque"). A spherical shape is considered the most beautiful. Round pearls are found inside mollusks and, according to Leonard Rosenthal in his book, *The Pearl Hunter*, owe their form to the facility with which they can move within the oyster. Pear-shaped pearls are formed by pressure "exerted by the edges of the shell." Button shapes and the irregular baroque shapes are found near the muscle of the oyster and are less sought after.

A pearl's color is very important. Colors vary through all shades of white. Many natural pearls have a yellowish-white or silver-white tinge. Pure white or pinkish white are considered the most desirable. The pinkish cast is exceptionally delicate when seen in combination with a shade of pure white. In his *Fourth Book of Airs* (1617), Thomas Campion wrote:

> Those cherries fairly do enclose
> Of orient pearl a double row,
> Which when her lovely laughter shows,
> They look like rosebuds fill'd with snow.

Pearls may also occur in fancy shades of blue, brown, green, pink, rose-pink, gray or black. Pearls have a quality called "luster" or "orient" which is the surface iridescence. As the layers of nacre grow, minute spaces are left between each layer. In a manner similar to the iridescence of opal, light is refracted between the layers. This orient, combined with fine "body" color, gives pearls their shimmering quality.

The finest natural pearls are perfectly spherical, having a whitish or slightly whitish-pink color, a fine luster, shiny orient and very great size. Ultimately, however, as with all gems, size is less important than quality. In 1661 Tavernier described a fabulous pearl:

> The Prince of Muscat, Asaf bin Ali, possesses the most beautiful pearl in the world, not by reason of its size, for it weighs only $12\frac{1}{16}$ carats, nor on account of its perfect roundness, but because it is so clear and so transparent that you can almost see the light through it.

Any pearl larger than 10 mm in diameter was and is still considered exceptionally rare. Naturally, to find a matched pair or, still harder, a layout for a necklace of matched pearls was believed a great prize. Although the Talmud lays down the margins of profit deemed proper and moral in every transaction, a matched pair of pearls was an exception to the rule, and a dealer could ask for them whatever he wished.

To the Romans, pearls were exceptionally valuable, too. Some Roman ladies in Nero's day would sleep on pearl-inlaid beds. In late Republican Rome (second century), sumptuary laws were enacted limiting the number of pearl necklaces that could be worn by an individual. There is a Byzantine mosaic showing the Emperor Justinian bedecked in pearls: he is shown wearing a sacred pearl cap that marks him out as the spiritual and temporal leader of Byzantium. Since early Christian times pearls have been regarded as symbolic of the Blessed Virgin Mary, as Jesus was believed to have been the great pearl she brought forth. Christian rulers would appear in their temporal office bedecked with pearls. Similarly, a ninth-century Byzantine medieval crown of the Holy Roman Empire, often called the "Crown of Charlemagne," has twelve precious stones surrounded by pearls. The twelve stones symbolize the twelve tribes of Israel, and the pearls as well as the pearl-studded cross stand for the purity and sacredness of faith.

In Renaissance times pearls were avidly sought for reasons of health. Rather than see a doctor, people would often turn instead to taking *aqua perlata*, ground-up pearl which, according to Anselmus de Boot, the leading lapidary of his day, was "most excellent for restoring the strength and also for resuscitating the dying." *Aqua perlata* was quite easy to make: Simply drop ground pearl into vinegar, add lemon juice, sulphur, a pinch of sugar, one ounce each of rose water, tincture of strawberries and balm, and two ounces of cinnamon water. And, as de Boot put it, "Shake well before using."

Round pearls were in enormous demand in the Renaissance. Queen Elizabeth I had thousands of them sewn into the sumptuous dresses that she wore at court. Each pearl would be sewn on in a criss-cross fashion and before the garment could be washed, the interlacing had to be removed and subsequently restitched. So great was her demand for pearls that thousands of imitation pearls were also bought by her (at a penny a piece) and sewn into her dresses. In *The Book of Pearls*, Joan Dickinson cites Horace Walpole's much later description of Elizabeth as she was portrayed in paintings:

> Elizabeth appears like an Indian idol, totally composed of pearls and necklaces. A pale Roman nose, a head of hair loaded with crowns and powdered with diamonds, a vast ruff, a vaster farthingale and a bushel of pearls are features by which everyone knows at once the picture of Elizabeth.

Baroque pearls were also much sought after. Venetian and southern German craftsmen would design jewels utilizing the basic shape of the baroque pearl. In her book *Renaissance Jewelry*, Yvonne Hackenbroch cites many examples of the ingenuity of Renaissance craftsmen in creating a jeweled object that was both gay and splendid. The Canning Jewel, in which the baroque pearl forms the torso of Triton, god of the sea, is an outstanding example in the Victoria and Albert Museum. Similarly, in Florence there exists a jewel that employs a baroque pearl as the body of a dragon being mounted by Virtue. This late sixteenth-century piece must have looked splendid indeed when worn by a Florentine noblewoman. Swinging on the end of a necklace, the baroque pearl, with its smooth, lustrous surface, would catch the light and this, with the brilliance of the ruby and the soft green of the enamel, combined to make the pendant a magnificent jewel.

In the early twentieth century, Leonard Rosenthal gives us an account of the pearl trade, which had not changed much over a period of two millennia. The Persian Gulf in 1908 (before the exploitation of oil resources) featured a group of sleepy fishing and smuggling ports. As in Tavernier's time, Arabs and Hindus did the diving and trading. While a fair amount of financing of stock purchases through English merchant banks took place, the pearl trade, by and large, was in the hands of Bombay traders. The crash of 1907–8 changed much of this. Rosenthal was able to send one of his brothers, Victor, to Bahrain where, with the help of Parisian banks, he established himself as the most important buyer in the Gulf. During the following twenty years, the important part of the pearl industry shifted to Paris. It was also a period of rapid inflation and the creation of many great American and European family fortunes. Pearls were the *sine qua non* of fashion and formed, along with a yacht, a mansion and a brace of polo ponies, part of the essential "kit" of the very rich. Frederick Kunz describes some of the fabulous prices paid for natural pearl necklaces. Mrs. William Astor, for example, would wear strands of pearls costing fifty thousand dollars then—the equivalent of a multi-million dollar necklace today. Pearls were figured on an intricate valuation system. The method of reckoning, logical at first glance, was in fact quite similar in an eerie kind of way to the "computerized price lists" that one sees for diamonds. After determining the relevant base price for pearls of a certain size, the weight of a pearl necklace was multiplied by the base price to arrive at a total price for the necklace.

Cultured pearls

In the 1920s Victor Rosenthal "accidentally" discovered, upon close examination, that a few of the pearls he had been buying were in fact cultured. It was only in the late 1920s, however, that pearls grown by artificial methods started to appear in great numbers on the market. The stage was thus set for a financial debacle in the pearl trade. In 1930, in a single day, sky-high prices for natural pearls came to an abrupt end. The Pearl Crash of 1930, as it is known in the trade, occurred when bankers refused to extend credit to pearl dealers on their stocks of cultured pearls. Pearl prices dropped by eighty-five per cent in a single day. This plunge was due to two factors: first, the Wall Street crash of 1929 completely undercut the purchasing power of wealthy buyers of natural pearls; secondly, the fact was that cultured pearls were coming onto the market in increasing numbers, and simply to distinguish the cultured from the natural variety was difficult at first. To understand this extraordinary Pearl Crash, one must look at the history of cultured pearls.

120 *A twentieth-century gold ring with a fine cultured pearl set into it. The shimmering luster of the pearl combines well with the warmth of the gold.*

121 (ABOVE) *A second-century Roman pearl necklace; because natural pearls lose their luster with the passage of time, it is difficult to guess how this necklace may have looked in its original form.*

122 The so-called Crown of Charlemagne, also known as the Reichskrone (Imperial Crown), preserved in the Hofburg, Vienna. The cross symbolized the "divine right" of the Holy Roman Emperor; the front panel features gemstones and pearls, while the arch bears a Latin inscription made with pearls.

123 Queen Elizabeth I. Like the Holy Roman Emperors, the English Queen used precious stones and pearls as objects of "political diplomacy." In her public appearances Elizabeth would be seen bedecked with precious stones and pearls, as here in the so-called "Ermine Portrait" attributed to William Segar, in order to give an overpowering impression of opulence and regal dignity.

124 (BELOW) *A Renaissance horse pendant, incorporating three highly lustrous natural pearls. The combination of the prancing horse with the brilliance of table-cut rubies and the use of delicate white enamel to mirror the whiteness of the pearls helps to make this pendant particularly lively when worn.*

125 (BELOW, RIGHT) *A sixteenth-century Venetian gold pendant. Natural pearls are utilized here, both for effect and to serve as the body of a mythical sea monster.*

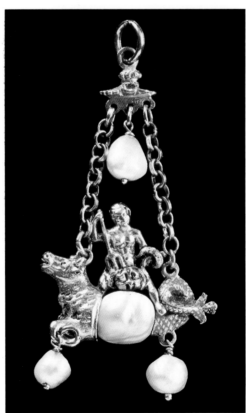

126 K. Mikimoto, who was a pioneer, both in culturing pearls and in making cultured pearls acceptable in jewelry circles throughout the world.

127 (RIGHT) Pinctada martensii, the host oyster used for the insertion of the pearl nuclei.

128 The insertion of nuclei is the most important and risky part of the pearl culturing process, and is the stage at which attention to detail is most needed; if any mistake is made, the culturing process will be aborted.

129 (ABOVE, LEFT) The oysters are kept inside cages, which are lowered into the shallow waters of *Ago Bay*.

130 (ABOVE) *Ago Bay*, formerly ideally suited to pearl culture, but now unfortunately becoming polluted as a result of industrialization; this development has materially contributed to the increased prices of cultured pearls.

131, 132 Amas, Japanese women pearl divers. Unlike the traditional *Arab* natural pearl divers, who were always men and boys, cultured pearl divers in Japan have always been women. On each dive they tend to stay down for less than a minute.

133, 134 Pearl sorting at Mikimoto's. Sorting is done with a view to blending together the color, luster and shape of all the pearls that make up a single strand.

135 (BELOW, LEFT) Grading irregular baroque pearls by shape and color.

136 (BELOW) Strands after being completely graded.

137 *A fine triple-strand necklace of uniform round pearls set in a high-fashion manner in a diamond necklace, with matching earrings.*

138 (BELOW, LEFT) *Pearls of various body colors ranging from grey-black, yellow, pink, pink-rose to cream.*

139 (BELOW RIGHT) *Cultured pearls of different shapes.* UPPER LEFT, *round pearls, suitable for necklaces;* UPPER RIGHT, *oval and pear-shaped freshwater pearls;* LOWER RIGHT, *freshwater treated black pearls;* LOWER LEFT, *a round pearl and a baroque shape, the latter being suitable for pendants or earrings.*

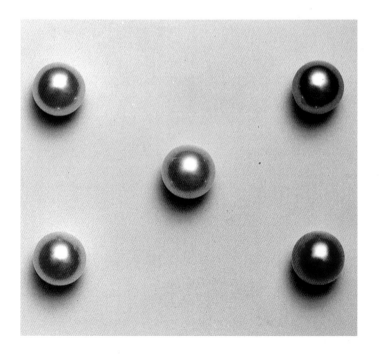

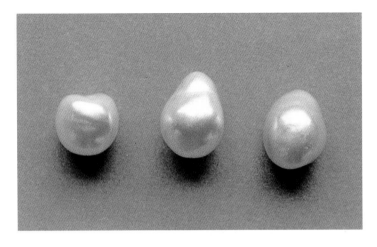

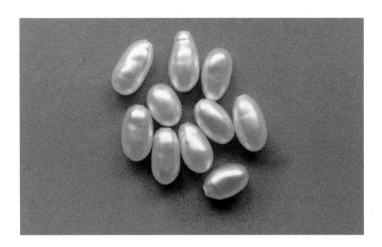

140 Baroque cultured pearl shapes; these have become very popular today for use in free-form jewelry.

141 A mabé pearl, ideal for setting into earrings.

142 Examples of freshwater pearls, from Lake Biwa in Japan and from Chinese fisheries.

143 Variations in color: the smaller pearl is cream, and the larger one whitish and tending to rose.

144 (RIGHT, ABOVE) An eighteenth- or early nineteenth-century Jaipur "Mughal"-style ring. Indian jewelers threaded seed pearls to give an effective border for a precious stone set in a ring.

145 (RIGHT, BELOW) The under-bezel of a mirror ring, Jaipur, nineteenth century. With such a ring a diffident Indian woman could, while seeming to avert her gaze, stare down at her hand and see a reflection of her husband. The crystal is bordered by threaded seed pearls.

146 *An extraordinary collection of natural undrilled Melo Royal Vietnamese Pearls.*

147 (ABOVE LEFT) *A modern necklace employing cultured pearls.*

148 (ABOVE RIGHT) *A necklace of natural black pearls. Recently, a method of naturally coloring cultured pearls to produce wonderful shades of black with greenish overtones has been developed. Tahitian pearls treated in this way have become much sought after by connoisseurs.*

149 *A black natural pearl necklace, accompanied by natural pearl drop earrings, surmounted with rose-cut diamonds. Natural pearl necklaces can be made up of pearls of all shades.*

150 *A gem-quality South Sea pearl necklace with very fine luster; the spherical pearls range from 11–14 mm in diameter. Each pearl is so closely matched in luster, cultivation and cleanness that the whole is an extremely rare necklace.*

As in so many other areas of invention, the Chinese were there first. Since the thirteenth century, the Chinese had placed tiny particles inside oysters to stimulate the growth of cultured pearls. As with firecrackers, however, once the Chinese had mastered the technique, they lost interest, and systematic experimentation did not follow initial technological success. It was the Japanese who perfected the cultivation of spherical pearls on a commercial basis. At the turn of the century Kokichi Mikimoto had started to experiment with pearl culture. He was not the only one in Japan working on this problem. He was probably not the first, either, for Tatsuhei, Mise and Nishikawa preceded Mikimoto in registering patents. In later years Nishikawa became Mikimoto's son-in-law. The question of who invented the cultured pearl therefore becomes somewhat academic. In any case, the genius of Mikimoto (originally a noodle vendor) lay in his remarkable skill in merchandizing cultured pearls. At first, French dealers tried to insist that cultured pearls should not be allowed to be described as "pearls," and lawsuits were instituted in Europe in an attempt to prevent the Japanese from marketing their creations as pearls. In the long run, however, cultured pearls have come to dominate ninety-five per cent of the pearl market today.

The Japanese method of cultivating pearls has depended upon many factors for its success. The first requirement is a large, shallow and calm body of water. In beautiful Ago Bay, near Ise, in eastern Japan, such a body of water exists, and it is here that tiny *Pinctada martensii* oysters are lowered onto rafts inside cages. After one year they are removed, cleaned and then put into new enclosures. Two years later the oyster shells are opened and tiny bits of mother-of-pearl as well as minute segments of mantle tissue (from living oysters) are placed inside the shell. Japanese skill in precision handiwork is justifiably renowned. Just as operations in the transistor industry and in the making of artificial flowers require painstaking patience and technique, so too does the insertion of the nuclei to produce cultured pearls. If the nucleus and the piece of mantle are placed in any position other than between the muscle and the internal organs of the parent oyster, the culturing process will be aborted. The oysters are left in this state for three-and-a-half years and require regular inspection.

Diving, both to place the oysters and to recover the oyster shells, is done entirely by Japanese women, known as *amas*. They wear white outfits and glass masks. Because of the shallowness of the bay, the *amas* need to stay under water generally for less than a minute for each diving operation. When, after several years, the oysters are removed from the shallow waters, they are opened and the cultured pearls are harvested. Then the cleaning and bleaching processes are started. The pearls are sorted very carefully by experts, for it is at this stage that a keen color sense and extraordinary sensitivity to shape are of key importance, since the blending of color and matching of like-shaped pearls are essential. Strands of cultured pearls are divided into the following "body" colors: white, rose, cream, yellow and gold. These categories are further subdivided into shades of overtone colors. In addition, black cultured pearls exist as a special category (*see opposite page*), these being unique to the waters off Tahiti.

Different countries show varying general color preferences: the United States for white pearls; Italy, rose; France, a cream variety of rose; Germany, a whitish but slightly pink color; and Brazil and other Latin American countries, a golden cream. These preferences are related to the predominant skin color of the inhabitants. Thus, golden and yellowish pearls will look absolutely stunning when worn by dark-complexioned people, whereas the fairer skin of northern Europeans seems to be brightened considerably by whitish-pink pearls.

The pearls are separated carefully according to size and shape. As with natural pearls, the most desirable cultured pearls are perfectly spherical. Egg shapes, drop shapes (like an elongated pear), pear shapes and flat button shapes are used for earrings or rings. Small pearls, with a diameter of under 3 mm, are called "seed" pearls, and an even smaller variety is called "dust" pearls. Although off-shaped baroque pearls have been less sought after than the spherical and rounded shapes, today's stylists are increasingly taking advantage of any suitable baroque shape to design a piece of jewelry that is both unique and fashionable.

In addition to body color and basic shape, the luster (or orient) is critical. If the layers of cultivation are too few, the cultured pearls will have no luster. In some instances in the past it has been possible almost to see the original nucleus in a cultured pearl. (Such an opportunity is virtually nonexistent today, however, as the Japanese Chamber of Commerce insists upon the destruction of poor-quality cultured pearls.)

In the Japanese blending system hanks of pearl strands (often thirty or forty strands) will be exported to one particular market. The pearls will tend to be of one body color, one overtone, a steady size and a constant shape. In the case of a strand of medium-luster, whitish pearls, their size will determine much of the value. An indication of current prices for a strand of pearls with a good color and good luster is shown in the table below. As already noted in the context of natural pearls, anything over 10 mm in diameter is rarely found among cultured pearls.

The copyrighted and trademarked system developed in the early 1990s by Mr. Kan Yue, a noted Far Eastern pearl expert, as used by my company, emphasizes the careful weighing of the parameters of pearl quality. First, pearls are described in terms of color: white, white-pink, cream, cream-pink and green. Next, a 1–5 scale for the intensity of color is used, with 1 being the lightest and 5 being the darkest. A "1 white-pink" would have a lot of white in it whereas a "5 white-pink" would be extremely pink. Next, cultivation of the pearl is rated on a 1–5 basis, with 1 being a very thin cultivation with very few layers of pearl, and 5 being a very thick cultivation with many layers of pearl. Next we have a 1–5 scale for luster: 1 would be a very dull shine, and 5 would be such a high luster that the pearls would begin to shimmer on the table. The last grading point is for cleanness: pearls rated 1 would be highly spotted goods, and 5 would be "eye-clean" goods.

At the same time, the physical dimensions of the pearls, the size in millimeters, the length of the strands, and the shape of the pearls (either round, oval, baroque, or semi-baroque) are described. If a pearl strand has high intensity, cleanliness, luster and cultivation, it will fit into the "AAA" quality. Medium-rated goods would be classified as "AA," and lower rated goods would be "A" quality. Naturally, to categorize pearls on the basis of intensity, cleanness, luster and cultivation requires a degree of connoisseur-ship. Once the proper categories are found, size is quite important. Today, typical prices for a limited number of strands would look like this:

Size (mm)	Price per strand ($) according to quality		
	A	AA	AAA
2 – 2½	480	600	680
2½ – 3	440	600	720
3 – 3½	400	600	720
3½ – 4	440	640	760
4 – 4½	400	600	800
4½ – 5	520	760	1,000
5 – 5½	600	840	1,040
5½ – 6	640	920	1,160
6 – 6½	660	1,100	1,500
6½ – 7	700	1,200	1,800
7 – 7½	800	1,800	2,400
7½ – 8	1,400	2,800	4,000
8 – 8½	2,400	4,000	6,000
8½ – 9	3,600	6,000	10,000

In general, it is not merely sellers' puff to say that the quality and quantities of pearls are declining rapidly. The total number being cultivated becomes smaller year by year, and the quality in most cases is not what it was even ten years ago. Environmental factors are the cause: Ago Bay and the Shimu Peninsula, as indeed most of Japan, are plagued by pollution. Industrialization has brought about a change in the character of Japan's once tranquil shallow waters. Chinese-made cultured pearls, although generally not completely round have competed in price with the Japanese strands.

Several methods of testing and differentiating between natural and cultured pearls have been used over the years. In the 1920s and '30s natural pearl dealers hired the French Nobel Prizewinner A. Perrin to figure out ways of distinguishing natural from cultured pearls. The apparatus he developed, the endoscope, was used to test pearls in which a drill hole had already been made; a powerful light beam was aimed through the drill hole, and, as natural pearls and cultured pearls have a different character to their centers, the path that the light took through the pearl was seen to be different. A pearl microscope, a lucidoscope and other devices were also used. Today, a very sophisticated technique is used by the Gemological Institute of America: X-ray pictures of natural pearls contrast with those of cultured pearls. As can be expected, the larger nuclei in cultured pearls distinguish them from the nuclei present in naturally formed pearls. This technique not only requires sophisticated machinery, however, but it is quite difficult to employ. It cannot be used by a non-specialist laboratory or by an ordinary pearl dealer.

Imitation pearls, however, can normally be separated from their cultured counterparts by the "tooth" test. To the trained connoisseur's tooth, imitation pearls feel smoother, whereas natural and cultured pearls have a gritty feel to them. Simulated pearls have a blotting-paper-like surface that is different from the ridged surface of nacreous pearl. In addition, there are on the market today very beautiful black cultured pearls that achieve their color through "natural" means. That is, cultured pearl nuclei are used in South Seas waters off Tahiti and come out after cultivation with lovely, lustrous shades of black. This process is an unusual combination of "man plus nature," in the sense that cultured pearls, after being inserted into the oysters, are carefully lowered into the Tahitian waters, where the next layers (which give rise to the distinctive color) are allowed to form over this rather large type of "cultured pearl seed."

There is a category of cultured pearls which has become increasingly popular today, namely, cultured pearls over 10 mm in diameter, known as South Sea pearls. As noted, cultured pearls from Japan very rarely reach 10 mm. However, both in the waters off Burma, as well as the waters off Australia, there are substantial fisheries producing strands of large South Sea pearls. Because of their remarkable size (these pearls range from 10 mm up to an occasional 22 mm), South Sea pearls make wonderful necklaces, rings, and other interesting jewelry designs. The Burmese South Sea pearls have a softer, somewhat pinkish cast to them, generally without a trace of green, whereas the Australian pearls have a more silvery look to them. Again, similar standards of intensity of color, cultivation, luster, and cleanness are all-important parameters of measuring quality.

It is not surprising that, given the enormous and increasing popularity of white South Sea pearls, that black South Sea pearls would come to be so sought after. Generally, a purchase of lustrous black pearls follows a purchase of South Sea white. Black is not truly a description of "black pearls," because, in fact, there are at least twenty different shades of peacock-black, bronze-black, greenish-black, pale gun metal-black, black so blue that one would be hard-pressed to call it black, and yet other extremely seductive mixtures of grey, black, blue, and green.

Choices between these various shades are truly personal ones. The producers of these various shades of black in the waters off Tahiti are not able to fine-tune the exact shade of the end pearl. Unlike a South Sea white pearl necklace, which should have a relatively uniform shade of white throughout the strand, black pearls can exhibit quite different shades of black from their neighboring pearls nestled in a necklace. The symphonic effect of mixing colors on a black strand often is breathtaking. The necklace can be worn again and again and in each light look quite different.

Auction houses currently provide a secondary market for cultured pearls, and even more so for South Sea pearls. South Sea strands of pearls with a diameter of 16 mm have sold at auction for sums between $25,000 and $1,000,000. Even larger sizes ranging up to 20 or 21 mm. have fetched multimillion-dollar figures. It is possible that cultured pearls will eventually come to be regarded in much the same light that natural pearls were in past centuries. However, it should always be remembered that the cultured pearl has its beginning through a "human hand." In times of great prosperity, the amount of pearls begun in the white and black pearl fisheries can be increased dramatically. This has led to periodic, sharp drops in prices of medium and lower-grade qualities.

While it is true that the white and black pearl producers, for example in the South Sea pearl farms off of Tahiti and Australia, have been one of the technological miracles of the 1990s, it is also true that output has been very often limited because of the ever-increasing degradation of the environment. Many of what would have been wonderfully-shaped and quite large collections have been decreased by as much as 50% because of environmental pollution.

As rare as findings of natural pearls in the Gulf was in the 1980s, natural pearl fishing was virtually stopped because of oil spills, as well as terrific chemical degradation of the Bahrain waters. One might, unfortunately, regard the natural pearl, and even to some degree the cultured pearl, as an endangered "species."

An exception to the concept of an endangered species would be the "buried treasure found" pearls. Several years ago, a collector walked into my office and opened a box containing twenty-three brilliant, natural orange pearls. James Traub describes them eloquently in "The Mystery of Origins," a chapter in *The Pearl and the Dragon: A Study of Vietnamese Pearls and a History of the Oriental Pearl Trade*, published in 1999 by the Gemological Institute of America as well as Mayney Press, England, and edited by Derek J. Content:

In a leather case, "arrayed in six lines like spokes of a wheel, were twenty-three brilliant orange pearls. Or rather, they looked more like pearls than anything else. They were not nacreous, with that sense of infinitely receding, oceanic depth which one expects to find in classic oyster pearls. They were as shiny as marble, though a whole world of lemony freckles and brownish ribbons swam just beneath their lustrous surface. Because they had not been drilled, and because many of them were almost perfectly spherical, they looked almost like machined objects. They looked, in fact, otherworldly. And they were enormous. The largest among them later turned out to measure 32 millimeters—bigger than a robin's egg."

After several years of investigation in libraries as well as in Vietnam itself, with the help of Kenneth Scarrett, a gemological and pearl expert, as well as with Derek J. Content, Thomas Moses, James Traub, and John Flattau, I've come to the conclusion that these pearls, unique as a collection, splendid in their beauty, are from a Vietnamese royal collection. These pearls, when turned gently on their axis, reveal a flame-like sun-spot pattern, just as the Chinese dragon symbol is perhaps related to some ancient discovered set of dinosaur bones somewhere in China, so too these pearls that come from the waters off of Vietnam and Thailand were probably the origin of the flaming pearl motif that appears so often as a symbol of perfect wisdom in Chinese art.

When this pearl collection was exhibited at the American Museum of Natural History, viewers could examine what James Traub described as an "otherworldly" beauty. There is always a chance that other treasure collections of natural pearls might surface; however, as years go on, such finds become more and more unusual.

Historic natural pearls, such as the Mancini Pearls sold in 1980 at Christie's (New York) for $230,000, fetch very high prices. In this particular case, the successful bid was approximately double the value the jewels would have commanded if no known history had been associated with them; as it was, this pair of earrings were of exceptional interest, for they had been a wedding gift to Queen Henrietta Maria, consort of Charles I of England, and had later come into the possession of Louis XIV of France.

Today, as emerald and diamond jewelry pieces are becoming increasingly expensive, items of pearl jewelry are being offered by retail stores at more affordable prices. Even so, as a result of increasing worldwide demand, combined with decreasing quantity and quality of supply, pearl prices have soared over the past few years. Besides the spherical forms, blister pearls, Biwa pearls, rice-shaped Chinese freshwater pearls (often in rainbow colors), baroque pearls, especially, and other exotic shapes are very much in favor, following trends in clothing fashions. The fashions of the 1950s and '6os, when black dresses and lower hemlines were common, encouraged the wearing of pearls. After the rather "wild" 1970s, when cultured pearls fell somewhat out of favor, more conservative trends in fashion are reappearing and pearls again have become very stylish. The 1980s were exceptionally good years for public demand for pearls, and the 1990s were positively nirvana for pearl dealers, advertisers, and marketers. Just as the 6½–mm. pearls became the staple for an elegant but no-nonsense executive look, the 15-mm. stunning South Sea white or black pearl necklace became the "don't-leave-your-home-without-it" for any Greenwich partygoer.

In a charming way, a Renaissance Medici thirst for pearls has come full circle, and, once again, pearls have joined the diamond, ruby, emerald, and sapphire at any sumptuous gathering.

Pearl care is extremely important. Pearls have a very long life if kept away from perfume and strong detergents. A gentle cleaning with a cloth will help to keep them in pristine condition. If this is done, one can expect that pearls bought by the present generation will still be worn with pleasure by the next. Time and again, pearls sold by the last generation of pearl dealers, when brought back for resale as "estate jewelry," very often have a yellowish cast, which the wearer of the pearl strand generally claims was not the case when the pearls were purchased thirty or forty years before. Again, we see that pearls are part of the world we all inhabit and are subject to the same inexorable ravaging of the environment.

Over the centuries pearls have had a broader appeal than any other gem, and given names associated with pearls occur more frequently than those associated with other gems. These personal names derive ultimately from the Greek word for pearl, *margaron*. Thus, in Italian, the name Margherita (or its abbreviated form Rita) is frequently encountered; in German, Gretchen and Gretel are diminutives of Margarete; in English, Margaret has maintained its popularity, even if often abbreviated, and of course Pearl itself is also used; and in French, Margot, from Marguerite, is a common given name.

151 An amber ring fashioned in Königsberg (now Kaliningrad) in the mid-nineteenth century.
"Specimen" pieces of amber were often mounted in low-grade silver rings and worn as amulets in
central and eastern Europe.

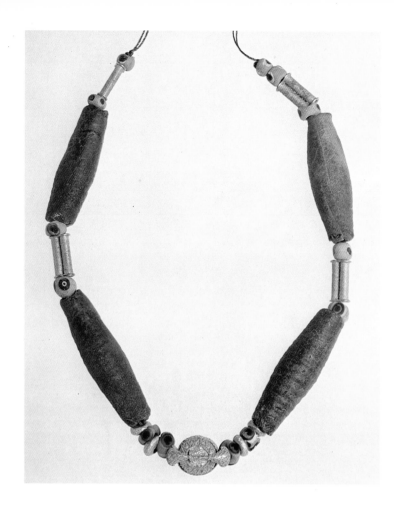

152-4 *An Etruscan amber bead necklace (seventh century* BC*). This piece illustrates the patination of amber that has occurred over a period of many centuries; it also contains a good example of Etruscan gold granulation around an Egyptian scarab. There is no doubt that the combination of the gold, the amber and the scarab was regarded as having a powerful aesthetic and religious significance for the wearer.*

155 *A Roman amber ring; this first-century hololith (a ring made entirely out of gem material) was regarded in ancient Rome as an especially powerful amulet.*

156 (BELOW) *An amber cup, fashioned in the second Bronze Age in England. Carved out of a single block of amber of Baltic origin, the cup exemplifies the ancient trade in amber as well as the technological skills of the Bronze Age carver.*

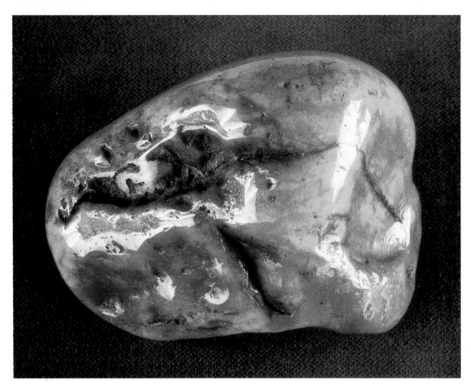

157 An amber boulder, not polished. A handsome specimen of this kind generally would have been cut into beads; occasionally, however, especially in nineteenth-century Germany, such amber boulders were exhibited as *objets trouvés*.

158 (BELOW) Depending upon the shape of the original amber pebble, beads can be fashioned in any form. Baltic amber may be highly translucent, as in the case of the light-yellow beads UPPER LEFT, or opaque or semi-opaque, as seen in the two pairs UPPER RIGHT and in the second pair on the left. The third pair down on the left is Persian amber, with a pleasing, muted, orange-brown color, much sought after in the Middle East. The bead on the lower left is Sicilian; it is greenish with an overglaze of blue, caused by the fluorescent property of amber from Sicily. The reddish so-called "Chinese" amber tends to occur as a flat bead, its flatness giving it an added translucency. The pair on the lower right is tomb amber, dating from Etruscan times.

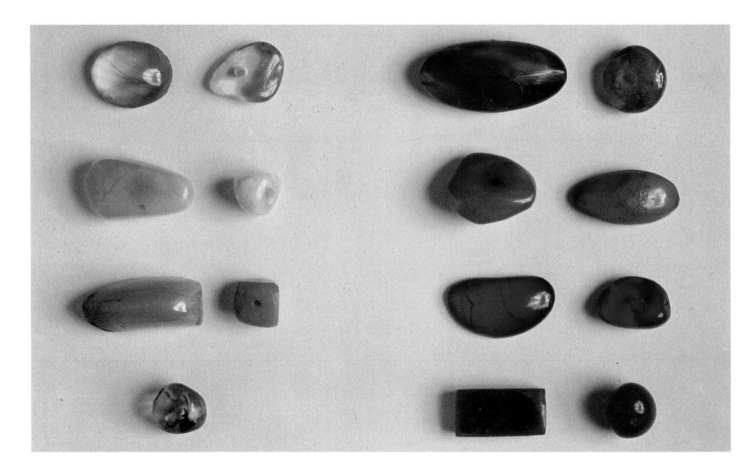

159 *A range of amber beads found in Etruscan tombs.*

160 Sicilian amber, the rarest type, exhibits fluorescence in varying degrees, creating an extraordinary play of color that is especially evident when the amber is worn in sunlight. Seen from one angle, the beads appear yellow, from another, a hazy blue.

161 *A brownish-yellow amber necklace, characteristic of the color of Baltic amber; the stringing is modern. Baltic amber accounts for the vast majority of amber necklaces. Although not translucent, the amber seen here is highly desirable to the European eye.*

162 *An estate jewelry amber piece, created from bits and pieces taken from many necklaces. In this piece there are examples of Burmese, Chinese, Rumanian, Baltic and Persian beads.*

163 *A very rare and highly desirable "Chinese" amber slab necklace, nineteenth century.*

164 (BELOW LEFT) Dark, honey-colored, Burmese amber in a necklace fashioned in the late nineteenth or early twentieth century; the clasp is modern.

165 (BELOW) *A necklace of Rumanian amber; while Rumanian amber and Baltic amber are often of a similar color, the Rumanian material tends to be more translucent.*

166 *Amber formed thousands of years ago occasionally contains trapped insects which, after alighting on the sticky resin, were enveloped and preserved in perfect condition.*

SEVEN

AMBER

"When a tiger dies, its spirit penetrates the earth
and becomes amber. Amber is called "hu-p'o," the
soul of the tiger.'

—LI SHIH-CHEN

AMBER COMBINES BOTH the elements of creation and the essence
of decay with the mystery of death and regeneration. Formed millions of years ago, it is the fossilized, solidified resin of certain
types of coniferous tree. In his excellent monograph *Gems and
Gemology*, Dr. Eduard Gübelin has pointed out that, although the largest concentration of amber is found along the Baltic coast, pine trees were not indigenous to the
area but originally grew in forests in Fenoscandia (Finland, Denmark, Norway and
Sweden). Over an enormous time period, the resin from these trees was wafted
across the Baltic Sea, finding its way to the coasts of Lithuania, Latvia, Russia and
Poland. The other principal sites for amber are Sicily, Rumania, Burma and the
Dominican Republic. Baltic amber is, however, different in color and character from
all of these other types; it occurs in all shades of yellow and honey-colored browns,
and vast quantities have been either mined or gathered from the sea bed for more
than three thousand years.

The three great periods of fashion for amber have been the Etruscan times, the
late Roman era and the Victorian age. Today, once again, amber is returning to favor
in high-fashion circles. In looking at an Etruscan amber piece of the sixth century
BC, now in the British Museum, one is struck by the mystery of amber. With their
fascination for death and the hereafter, the Etruscans endowed the deceased with
costly tomb jewelry—for men and women. They were able to import Baltic amber
from over two thousand miles away and fashion beads to be made into necklaces

for use in burials. These beads are known to be of Baltic origin, and not from the geographically closer Sicilian amber mines, because Baltic amber has a characteristic chemical composition: scientifically, it is called "succinite" because it contains a high concentration of succinic acid (five to eight per cent). Over the centuries Baltic amber grows darker and takes on a patina of brownish red, first from the outside and, eventually, throughout the piece. Thus, while newly mined Baltic amber looks yellowish, the objects excavated from Etruscan tombs have a darker appearance. Both of the necklaces now in the British Museum were discovered by intrepid Italian tomb robbers in the nineteenth century. The pieces were purchased by that remarkable Italian goldsmith, Fortunato Pio Castellani (1793–1865), and his son, Alessandro. These pieces were a source of inspiration to the Castellanis, who, after careful study, succeeded in duplicating the Etruscan technique for producing granulated gold and filigree work. Eventually, Alessandro Castellani donated many of his Etruscan-style treasures to the British Museum, but there is some dispute about the origins of a few of those pieces—some may be Castellani's own work, "artfully" patinated by him in imitation of antique originals.

How was amber recovered by the people of the Baltic region in the sixth century BC? Basically, the same method was used until the eighteenth century. Men and women would wade for long hours just beyond the shoreline at low tide, using spears to loosen the amber boulders embedded in the sea-floor. In one hand they would hold a spear; with the other hand, a net would be employed to scoop up the amber. The amber boulders recovered from the sea would then be cut with a slow-turning bow drill.

The Etruscan fascination with death and life after death found expression in amber because of its inclusion pattern. Over millennia, the constituent resin, being sticky, would act as environmental "fly paper." To one who knows how to read its secrets, amber provides a diary of the climate, and the flora and fauna of Fenoscandia. For example, a butterfly inclusion (that is the tip of a butterfly's wing that was trapped and preserved in the resin that became amber) tells us that a certain type of butterfly existed long ago. Often, entomologists will identify such a butterfly as an extinct species. The fact that butterflies frequently appear in amber shows us that the pine trees from which the amber in question came stood close to open meadows characteristic of butterfly habitat. Portions of palm-tree leaves have also survived in amber, showing, surprisingly, that Fenoscandia was once semi-tropical, with a climate quite similar to that of the Caribbean today.

The presence of large numbers of insects in Baltic amber is evidence of the existence of swamps at various times. Often, a mosquito would alight on the amber resin and would be entombed and preserved forever in the pose of death. To the Etruscan mind, these "frozen" life forms served as talismans to protect and mummify a deceased person for all eternity.

The Romans, especially the Emperor Nero, had a fabulous love for amber. An amber boulder was worth more than "a group of healthy slaves." Nero, that peculiarly Roman aesthete, loved amber because its color matched the color of his wife's hair. (As was the fashion in Rome, many of the ladies in Nero's court dyed their hair to match his aesthetic standards.) Amber objects dating from late Roman times have been shown also to be of Baltic origin. The Amber Road, from the Baltic to Rome, was one of the important trade routes of early antiquity. Those who supplied amber from northern Europe would on arrival barter the raw material in exchange for Roman "manufactured" goods.

Amber has also been found in Rumania, where the color tends to run toward a translucent shade of yellow and brown. In the Middle Ages and the Renaissance, both Baltic and Rumanian amber were "turned" (fashioned) by skilled craftsmen into *objets de vertu*. Amber-turning guilds were very important in the Renaissance economy. Jeweled caskets, chess sets and many other objects were fashioned. The culmination of amber craftsmanship was the creation, in the late eighteenth century, of the Amber Room, an entire chamber with walls of amber, glistening and translucent. This was the fanciful creation of King Frederick William I of Prussia. The huge chunks of amber necessary to line entire walls in this way were obtained by improved amber mining technology along the Baltic coast. Instead of picking at the surface of the coastline, hundreds of miners sank shafts into the ground and were thus able to recover relatively large chunks of the material. The Amber Room itself vanished mysteriously in 1945. In her book, *Amber*, Rosa Hunger states that, during the closing days of World War II, the retreating Germans probably dismantled the room. It is believed to have been looted by the Soviet army and it is possible that it still exists today somewhere in Eastern Europe.

Sicilian amber is one of the glories of nature. Intensely fluorescent in sunlight, it appears reddish brown, greenish and, occasionally, blue. Virtually every color occurs in Sicilian amber. Today, however, the supply of amber from Sicily has been exhausted. Pieces turn up, from time to time, in estate jewelry and are avidly sought after by amber connoisseurs.

Burmese amber tends to be a darkish, honey-brown, often quite lustrous and translucent. Amber from Burma was imported into China and "turned" there into necklaces, bracelets and rings. China has had a long technological history of importing precious materials—jade, rubies, and sapphires—from Burma and Ceylon, and then having its skilled lapidaries turn the rough material into exquisitely fashioned jewelry. So-called "Chinese" amber in fact originates in Burma. It is reddish and, because of its luster, appears to shimmer in the sunlight; it is often cut in flat, rectangular slabs. The red color is much sought after.

Another important source of amber was Rumania. This variety, called roumanite, is generally a dark, brownish yellow, but is more transparent than the Baltic type. Rumanian amber is quite rare and found only in estate pieces, as the mines are virtually exhausted today.

Persian amber, an orange-brownish substance, tends to be quite opaque. This property is often exploited by Persian craftsmen, who facet amber into intriguing box-like beads. However, the largest source, by weight, of amber today is the Dominican Republic, although the material is not much appreciated by connoisseurs. This newcomer is an almost blackish shade of brown. As the other major amber sources have become exhausted, however, Dominican amber probably will achieve increasing acceptance.

In her excellent and definitive book, *Amber, The Golden Gem of the Ages*, Patty Rice cites the theory that different species of trees are responsible for the different shades of color seen in material from widely separated sources. Baltic amber was formed by pine trees, while greenish amber may have been formed by spruce trees and the reddish variety by cherry trees. Previously, a particular shade in amber had been thought to result from the inclusions present in it.

In Great Britain, during the Victorian era, with its extraordinary emphasis on memorial jewelry and articles of remembrance (especially after the death in 1861 of the Prince Consort), amber was much prized. Demand vastly exceeded supply and, as a result, large numbers of imitations came into being. Substitutes were copal, a resin quite similar to amber, as well as a variety of plastics. An early twentieth-century invention of Leo Baekeland, Bakelite, presents a remarkably close imitation; similarly, glass has frequently been used to simulate amber. Pieces of genuine amber (especially the Dominican variety), can be fused together by being heated and subjected to pressure, to form amberoid.

By using a microscope, a fluorescent machine or a hot point, it is possible to distinguish genuine amber from its substitutes. Viewed through a microscope, gas bubbles in amber appear circular, while in pressed amber they tend to be elongated and oval. When touched with a hot point, amber gives off a characteristically resinous odor, whereas Bakelite emits an acrid smell. (Because the hot-point test is destructive, it should of course be applied to an inconspicuous part of the amber bead, and then only by an expert.) Glass substitutes are harder and heavier than natural amber and, more importantly, glass is cold to the touch, whereas amber, an organic substance, feels warm. When bitten, amber, like pearl, gives the teeth a gritty feeling, a quality that takes a degree of expertise to detect. Plastics and glass "taste" different from amber. Finally, the specific gravity of amber is 1.08, lighter than that of most amber substitutes.

The value of amber depends upon its shade of color. To the European sensibility, color is the most important factor. Even "fatty" amber, or "bastard" amber, a semi-opaque type, is desirable if it has fine color. To Americans and other new connoisseurs, however, translucence seems to be the most important aesthetic requirement. To the American eye, the more transparent the amber, the more desirable it is. Fine amber necklaces today are quite rare and are generally obtained in stores or auction houses specializing in estate jewelry.

Amber's name itself has been suggestive of the different cultural standards of various people throughout the ages. To the scientific Greek mind, in antiquity, the fascination of amber lay in its property to attract through static electricity. The Greeks called it *elektron*, from which also the word electricity and its many related forms are derived. (The only gemstone mentioned by Homer was amber.) To the Arabs, with their trader's sense of where things come from, the word for amber and for the totally unrelated ambergris was the same—because both substances happened to come from the sea and to be washed ashore. The German word *Bernstein*, "burning stone," emphasized the properties distinguishing amber from other substances, especially the peculiarly resinous odor it gives off when heated (like incense). The Lithuanians called amber *gintras*, from a root word meaning "protection," because to the Lithuanian way of thinking, amber protects the wearer from the perils of life.

Amber goes in and out of fashion. Its color has an uncanny ability to capture and alter light. The interior of amber is a diary of the past, and there are some amber collectors who acquire the material on the somewhat esoteric basis of its insect inclusions. Given its variety and interest, it is not surprising that amber continues to be much treasured by gem connoisseurs today.

EIGHT

LAPIS LAZULI

O my sister Inanna,
For Erech let the people of Aratta artfully fashion gold and silver;
Let them take pure lapis lazuli from the slab;
From the high land let them bring down the stones of the mountains;
And build for me a great shrine.

From a Sumerian cuneiform tablet, c. 2500 BC

FROM THE STANDPOINT of the Sumerians, nearly five thousand years ago, it would be difficult to imagine a point more remote than the lapis mines in mountainous Afghanistan, far from their own city of Uruk, the center of Sumerian culture in southern Mesopotamia. In the sacred tale, "The Descent of Inanna," the mother-goddess of Sumer descends to the underworld. Diane Wolkstein and Samuel Noah Kramer, in *Inanna—Queen of Heaven and Earth* (1983), include this description of her descent:

She places the shugurra, the Crown of the Steppe, on her head;
She ties her lapis lazuli beads around her neck . . .
And takes her lapis lazuli measuring rod and line in one hand.

From this one can readily see the centrality of lapis lazuli to the Sumerian mind, and it comes as no surprise therefore that in the early 1920s, when the royal tombs of Ur were excavated by Sir Leonard Woolley in what is now eastern Iraq, wonderful examples of lapis funerary jewelry and artifacts were discovered inside most of them. Many of the treasures recovered are now in the Iraq Museum in Baghdad. The

151

contents of the tomb of Queen Pu-abi (c. 2600 BC) are on display at the British Museum and at the University of Pennsylvania. They include a crown made up of gold leaves intersected by a band of lapis lazuli beads; hanging from the lapis beads are lapis "eyes," while at the very top of the crown are three stars. Around the queen's neck is a lapis choker and at least seven strands of lapis roundels. We thus have the symbolism of the stars in heaven (Inanna was regarded as the Queen of Heaven), growth on earth, symbolized by the leaf motifs of gold, and the riches beneath the surface of the earth, symbolized by the lapis. Lapis was believed to be the gift of the heavens to the people of Sumer.

Because of the difficulties in transporting lapis over vast distances, it is not surprising that only the finest-quality material was deemed worthy of being carried. On studying the treasures found in the royal cemetery of Ur, one is struck by the beauty of the objects fashioned from lapis. The finest Sumerian seals are made of carved lapis lazuli, and one such seal (in the Ashmolean Museum in Oxford) bears the seven-pointed rosette of Inanna, with an eye motif as well as Inanna herself standing under the moon. No magnificent jewelry, no crown and no princely bracelet would have been complete without some lapis. The finest ring—of lapis, carnelian and gold -excavated from Ur (from Lagash) is now on display in the Louvre.

Often, lapis was used as a veneer inlay. The so-called standard of Ur, for example, presents an imaginative use of flat lapis to create a mosaic effect. In low-lying Mesopotamia, the intense blue of lapis was equated with the vast expanse of blue sky and hence was greatly revered. Even after the long trek from Afghanistan to Sumer, the painstaking, careful fashioning of lapis into royal jewelry probably took many more years. The result, however, is breathtaking in its splendor, and the repeated poetic references to lapis occurring in cuneiform inscriptions provide ample evidence of its importance in that ancient civilization.

Lapis is not a specific mineral. It is, more precisely, a type of rock, a combination of minerals. It is composed primarily of lazurite, with small included admixtures of pyrite (the shiny, glittering specks of "gold"), calcite and diopside. The name "lapis lazuli," meaning "stone of azure," is based on the Latin *lapis* (stone) and the Arabic word meaning "sky blue"—*allaz ward*. This word was transposed in Latin to *azura*.

The only known source of lapis in the second millennium BC was Badakhshan. In the early 1960s Georgina Hermann of Oxford led a group of historians on a visit to the Badakhshan source, in a remote corner of northeastern Afghanistan. Even by

167 *A Sassanian ring (sixth century) containing an inlaid lapis seal. The seal on the ancient Persian ring was a "house mark," a symbol for a family, often illiterate. The knob on the top of the ring indicates the correct orientation when the seal was impressed.*

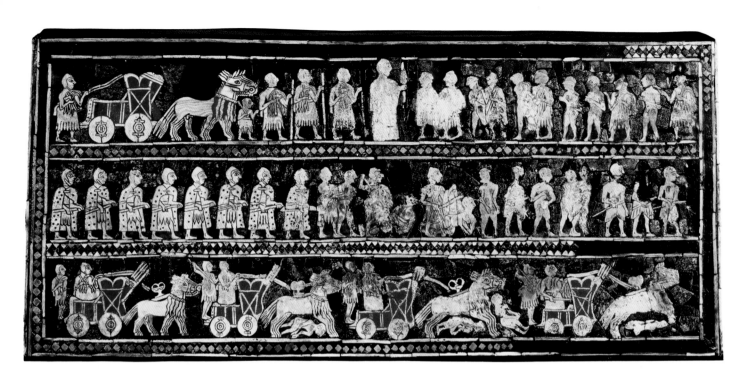

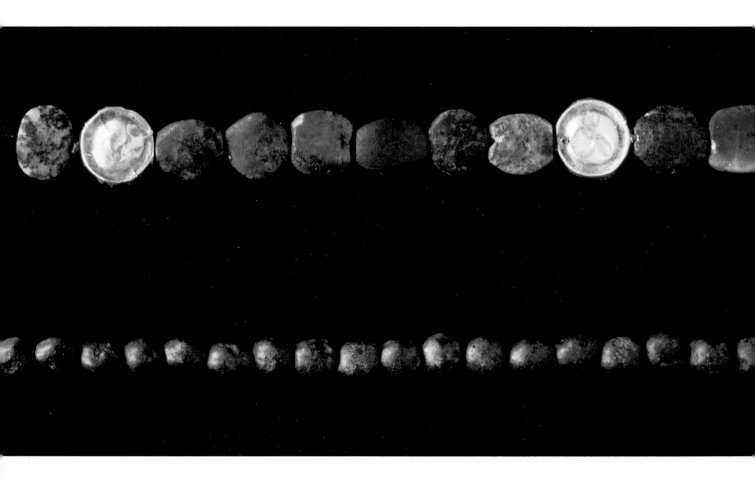

168 (LEFT, ABOVE) The "Royal Standard" of Ur, an oblong box about 18 in. (45 cm) long was discovered in the course of Sir Leonard Woolley's excavations and now in the British Museum. In a delicate lapis mosaic inlaid with gold, "War" and "Peace" are depicted on the opposite long sides, the former (shown here) symbolized by horsemen and chariots, and "Peace" by processions of servants and domestic animals and—in the upper register —a court banquet with musical accompaniment.

169 (LEFT, BELOW) Two necklaces from Sumer, made from Afghan lapis beads. It is not known whether the lapis was cut into bead form in Afghanistan or transported in the rough form to Sumer and cut there, but considering the length and the difficulty of the journey, it is probable that the beads were fashioned near the original source.

170 The reconstructed crown from the tomb of Queen Pu-abi (c. 2600 BC), in which lapis and gold are combined in a striking way. The roundel form of the lapis seen here is still in vogue today; French dealers find their Middle Eastern clients enamored of these shapes. The crown, preserved in the British Museum, represents a symbolic short-hand, suggesting the power of the queen over heaven, the earth and the riches beneath the surface of the earth.

171 "The Month of May," from the Da Costa Hours; in this page from a Bruges manuscript dating from 1515 (now in the Pierpont Morgan Library, New York [M. 399, f. 6v.]), the lute-playing lady is shown wearing a blue dress, the color of which resulted from the use of ground, powdered lapis. The paler shade of blue used in depicting the horseman—less dramatic and less noble—seen in the distance is derived from azurite.

172 *A scribe preparing and blocking out a Bible. In this thirteenth-century manuscript illuminated in Paris (now Pierpont Morgan Library, New York [M. 240, f. 8]), ground lapis was used to achieve the "gem-like" blue of the scribe's coat. In medieval times a contract for this type of work would often stipulate the use of lapis blue.*

173 (BELOW) *A Latin manuscript Psalter featuring the use of azurite (French, c. 1320): "For the fool hath said in his heart, 'There is no God'" (Psalm 14,1). Here, we see that the fool's dress is appropriately rendered, not in lapis blue but in azure.*

174 *An unusually large and fine Russian tazza (c. 1845); Russian lapis tends to have more calcite veining and more pyrite than Afghan material. Although, generally, Afghan lapis has a richer, deeper blue color, some gem Russian lapis is indistinguishable from the Afghan material.*

175 (BELOW) *Two fine intaglios set in rings. LEFT, Hercules wrestling with the giant Antacus—son of Poseidon and Earth (Ge)—who, while in contact with his mother (the ground) remained invincible and could only be overcome by being held in mid-air; here, the subject is depicted in blue glass in imitation of lapis.* RIGHT, *a natural blue lapis with pyrite inclusions, set in a Migration period ring.*

176 *A Fabergé figure of a coachman; the renowned jeweler created this figure in lapis lazuli, together with aventurine quartz for the face and hands, obsidian for the hair and beard, and a dull-black slate for the hat (containing the initial "I" for isvoschik, the Russian word for coachman). The color and luster of the lapis give the coachman's coat an extraordinary liveliness.*

177 *An oval box in silver, gilt and enamel, mounted in lapis lazuli and rock crystal; Viennese, nineteenth century.*

178 (BELOW) *An eighteenth-century inlaid lapis box; in the handling of the inlay the whitish calcite inclusions are used imaginatively to give the box a cottony, cloud-like appearance.*

179 (BELOW) *A group of lapis lazuli objects.* LEFT: *a late nineteenth-century box set with diamonds and pearls, in which the lapis is of an extraordinary saturated color, not too dark and not too light; set by Fried & Koechli for Fabergé, the box was formerly in the collection of the Grand Duchess Xenia of Russia.* RIGHT: *examples of Siberian lapis, more included and not of as good a color.*

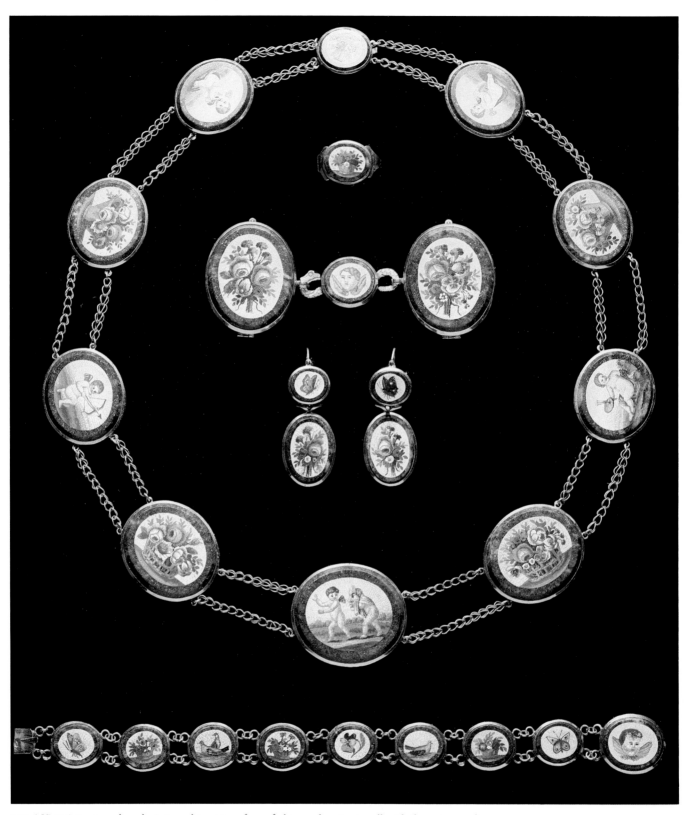

180 *A Victorian parure; here, lapis is used in picture-frame fashion and contrasts well with the center panels.*

Afghan standards, Badakhshan is easily the most treacherous, inhospitable and majestic of all gem sources. In her article "Lapis Lazuli: The Early Phases of Its Trade," Georgina Hermann describes the swiftly flowing rivers that have cut deep canyons and gorges into the mountains in the Kerano-Munjan valley. In the mountains at Sar-i Sang, approximately 17,000 feet (5,500 m) above sea-level, the original source for lapis is to be found.

The mines were accessible for only a few months of the year when the icy passes were negotiable. In fact, the trail is so narrow that for stretches it is impossible to take a horse, and one has to proceed on foot, using leather strips to protect one's feet and a walking stick to help traverse the deep pits and crevices. In its manual "Lapis Lazuli," the Gemological Institute of America describes how an English traveler to this area was told, "If you wish not to go to destruction, avoid this narrow valley." For her part, Georgina Hermann describes the Badakhshan mining areas—with masterly understatement—as "difficult." Even the Afghan miners are terrified of these mines on the roof of the world, and it is not unusual for the traveler to have a guide who has never seen the actual mine but has only heard tales about it.

Mining for lapis lazuli is extremely primitive and the method has not changed substantially since antiquity. Lapis occurs in veins embedded in marble, and the host rock is heated by means of fires started directly under the marble deposit. Then, water from melted snow is thrown onto the heated rock, which immediately cracks. In this way ten- to twenty-pound (4.5–9 kg) pieces of lapis may be recovered and then sent out through the narrow mountain paths to Pakistan (Lahore).

In Sumerian times lapis was sent westward and southwestward to the Indus River civilizations at Harappa, Mundigak and through Susa to Ur and Uruk. A poem translated by S. N. Kramer—"Enmerkar and the Lord of Arata"—tells of the land east of Sumer where "lapis lazuli is extracted from the rocks." Although there are no datable settlements from the Sumerian period in Badakhshan, sites are now being excavated that might provide proof of lapis export at that time.

In modern times other sources for lapis have been exploited as well as Afghanistan. Russian or Siberian lapis comes from near Lake Baikal, just across the border from Afghanistan. These mines too are very inaccessible, close as they are to the Pamir Mountains and the mighty Amu-Darya (the Oxus River of antiquity). Russian lapis has more pyrite in it than the Afghan material and also the rock is marked by frequent calcite veining. It generally does not approach in quality the best, deep bluish, slightly violet Afghan lapis, considered the finest in the world, although some Russian lapis is indistinguishable from the Afghan material. Russian lapis mines were largely exhausted by the nineteenth century so that Afghanistan, once again, is now the only source for gem lapis. In Chile, north of Santiago, a large source of lapis exists, but the material is softer, marked by a greenish tinge, and is not much sought after by connoisseurs.

In the Middle Ages lapis again came into great demand, for among devout Christians nothing was more magical than the blue mantle of the Virgin. In richly decorated illuminated manuscripts executed in Bruges and in northern Italian cities (the finest centers of medieval art), we find contracts between great patrons and the manuscript illuminators. Wherever the finest manuscripts were commissioned, "lapis blue" was insisted upon.

How was lapis ground up to yield the blue color? In a description by the painter Cennini that served as a fourteenth-century guide to manuscript illumination, the following formula, quoted by Daniel V. Thompson in *Materials and Techniques of Medieval Paintings*, is given:

To begin with, get some lapis. Pound it in a bronze mortar, covered up so that it may not go off in dust. . . . Work it up without water. Then take a covered sieve such as the druggists use for sifting drugs, and sift it over again as you find necessary. Bear in mind that the more finely you work it up, the finer the blue will come up but not so beautifully violet in color. . . . When you have got this powder all ready, get six ounces of pine turpentine from the druggist, three ounces of mastic and three ounces of new wax for each pound of lapis lazuli. . . . Melt them up together. Then take a white linen cloth and strain these things into a glazed basin . . . of linseed oil and always keep your hands well greased. . . . When you want to extract the blue from it, make two sticks . . . squeeze and knead the plastic mixture. When the lye is saturated with blue, draw it off into a glazed porringer. . . . Do this for several days in the same way until the plastic will no longer color the dye. . . . Be prudent in your observation not to spoil the fine blues . . . and keep this to yourself, for it is an unusual ability to know how to make it properly. Know too that making it is an occupation for pretty girls rather than for men, for they are always at home and reliable, and they have more dainty hands. Just beware of old women.

The lapis blue pigment that resulted from the process described by Cennini came to be known as "ultramarine" ("from across the sea"—a literal reminder of its origin), and Thompson states that "to follow Cennini's advice and exhibit this beautiful and costly color in conjunction with metallic gold was to reach the peak of highest elegance in appearance, in associations and in intrinsic worth."

Lapis became the ultimate symbol of elegance. In looking at the radiant colors in one of the Pierpont Morgan Library's prize possessions—"The Month of May," from the Da Costa Hours, a Bruges manuscript (c. 1515)—one realizes how wise the northern European patron was to insist upon lapis, and only lapis, as the coloring agent for the blue. One leading authority, Professor Harry Bober, has described the "jewel-like quality" of the medieval illuminators' work. Their blues as well as the reds and greens have a purity of color associated both with gems and with the finest medieval stained-glass windows. Indeed, the illuminator's sensitivity to color is comparable to the eye of a jeweler. Simon Bening, one of the illuminators of "The Month of May" manuscript, portrays a very elegant Bruges lady sitting in a rowboat heralding the month of May. Her cloak, in the purest shade of lapis blue, is cunningly mirrored in a blue reflection in the water. In the background is a figure, wearing a light-blue robe, astride a horse. He is less important than the lady, for the blue of his robe is azure, not a lapis blue.

In another masterpiece owned by the Pierpont Morgan Library, a thirteenth-century Parisian moralized Bible, lapis blue is chosen as the "royal" color of the cloak of a bending scribe; here, the reason for its use is that, because the scribe is writing a sacred text and the text flows through him, he is considered noble. Again, both the rarity of the lapis color and the ecclesiastical quality of the blue echo the rarity and sacredness of the biblical message.

When less aristocratic tastes prevailed, other blue colorings—azure blue, indigo blue or artificial copper blue—were used. Azure came from a copper ore and in medieval times was termed the "Armenian stone," azurite. This blue was available from mines in France, Germany and Hungary. Azurite, however, does not have the slightly purple, deep royal-blue characteristics of lapis. Seen under a microscope, azurite crystals are more uniform than their lapis counterparts. A Latin manuscript Psalter (French, c. 1320) shows the use of azurite in a figure placed alongside the text of Psalm 14, verse 1: "The fool hath said in his heart, 'There is no God.'" The illuminator might have thought that it was inappropriate to give the fool a lapis-colored coat and thus depicted him in a less rich shade of blue, using azurite. Indigo blue, a vegetable dye, and artificial copper blues did not have the color of and, more importantly, were not as permanent as, ultramarine—lapis lazuli.

The third great age of lapis, after its central use in antiquity and in medieval Europe, came in the late-nineteenth and early-twentieth centuries. Peter Carl Fabergé (1846-1920), of the House of Fabergé, should be regarded as following in the tradition of the great medieval European craftsmen. He was easily the greatest jewelry maker of the nineteenth century. His ancestors were of French Huguenot stock and had left France because of the persecution of Protestants. They settled in Russia, and Fabergé set up a constellation of factories to fashion incredibly intricate, well designed and perfectly crafted jewelry. His genius lay in encouraging talented workmen from all over Europe to settle in Russia. He enabled Finns, Letts, Slavs, Hungarians, Frenchmen and Italians to emigrate and set up ateliers. Fabergé did not own these factories but rather provided them with the materials with which to fashion jewelry. They in turn would supply him on an exclusive basis.

In 1884, Fabergé sold a jeweled Easter egg to Tsar Alexander III, and for decades afterward he became the purveyor of fabulous jeweled fantasies to royalty and the upper classes throughout Europe. Over seven hundred people worked on clocks, watches, rings, necklaces, brooches and *objets d'art* in these satellite workshops. Fabergé's sensibility was entirely different from that of his rival, Cartier. Cartier's style placed a great emphasis on the use of precious stones—rubies, sapphires, emeralds and diamonds—whereas Fabergé used these stones only occasionally. The worth of his creations did not depend upon the intrinsic value of the stones themselves. Quite the contrary, Fabergé, a true aesthete, sought to create beauty himself. He preferred working with less costly stones (and even invented some gem-imitation materials). Fabergé personally chose each and every stone used in all of the jeweled objects created in his workshops. He inspected each piece to ensure that it matched the high standards of the House of Fabergé. Indeed, the tale of Fabergé's smashing with a hammer any pieces that did not meet his exacting standards is not an apocryphal one. This system, which does not seem to be in accord with modern psychological techniques of support and encouragement, nevertheless produced jewelry of the highest possible standard of workmanship.

One of Fabergé's greatest loves was lapis. In the early years of the present century, he created a naturalistic figurine of a coachman, so solid, so powerful looking, and yet so obsequious that it seems more like a photograph than an *objet d'art*. Only

3⅝ in. (92 mm) high, this study in blue has a remarkable, child-like charm. The genius of the piece lies in the inventive use of lapis, for, far from regarding the pyrite inclusions as a flaw, Fabergé emphasizes them as an aesthetic adumbration of the gilt buttons and belt. The tiny coachman is all brightness. Velvety lapis gives a flowing quality to the coat, which in turn suggest the coachman's overflowing physique barely contained by his enameled belt.

Fabergé also inlaid many boxes (as well as picture frames) with lapis, in the tradition of eighteenth- and nineteenth-century lapis inlay work. Great care was always taken to ensure that the color, texture and inclusions of the specific piece of lapis were appropriately emphasized. Originally created for individual clients, many of these pieces have since found their way into museum collections, where they can now be viewed and enjoyed by a wide circle of lapis connoisseurs.

The enormous difficulty in obtaining supplies of lapis led to various attempts to simulate it. In one case jasper was stained blue and called "Swiss lapis"; no pyrite inclusions are present in this material, although flakes of quartz are sometimes mistaken for pyrite. Occasionally, opaque glass is produced containing shiny copper crystals, but these crystals can be separated by microscopic analysis, indicating the presence of gas bubbles. Lapis itself is often dyed to improve and deepen its blue color. It will lose its dye, however, with the application of acid. Genuine lapis will fluoresce slightly under longwave ultraviolet light, although more precisely it is the calcite inclusions that are actually fluorescing (pale pink) while the lapis itself is inert. Lapis is sometimes imitated by sodalite which, while somewhat similar in color, tends to be more violet and never contains pyrite. The specific gravity of sodalite is considerably higher than that of lapis, and thus helps to distinguish it.

Because of its opaque nature, lapis has rarely been faceted and down the ages has generally been fashioned into cabochon or bead forms, or used as an inlay. Extremely difficult to obtain, coming from the rooftops of the world, and splendidly blue, lapis provides a link between the eye and the remote royal reaches of the night sky.

NINE

JADE

"When I think of a wise man, he seems like jade. Wise men have seen in
jade all different virtues. It is soft, smooth and shining like kindness. It is
hard, fine and strong like intelligence. Its edges seem sharp but do not
cut, like justice. It hangs down to the ground like humility. When struck,
it gives a clear, ringing sound, like music. The stains in it, which are not
hidden and which add to its beauty, arc like thoughtfulness. Its brightness
is like heaven while its firm substance, born of the mountains and the
waters, is like the earth. That is why wise men love jade."

—Quoted by JOAN M. HARTMAN, in *Chinese Jade of Five Centuries*,
from the *Shih-ching* (Book of Poetry), c. AD 800

JADE MAY BE either of two distinct types of mineral: nephrite and jadeite.
Today, what we think of simply as jade—the bright emerald-green material that one sees displayed in museum cases and occasionally in windows on Fifth Avenue or on Bond Street—is jadeite. This comes from
Burma, has a hardness of 6.5 to 7 measured on the Mohs' scale; (on this scale the
highest number, 10 = the hardness of diamond) and, if carefully polished, exhibits
a wonderful luster.

Jadeite was first imported into China during the Ch'ing Dynasty, late in the
eighteenth century. Before that, the mineral described as "jade" was in fact nephrite.
Nephrite occurs in the same colors as jadeite, but the colors of the former are generally more muted in tone; nephrite appears to be soapy and somewhat lustrous. To
the Chinese eye, however, both materials are considered beautiful in different ways.

To see the difference between the minerals, let us compare two pieces that were
on display at the Asia Society in New York, in an exhibition called "Chinese Jades
from Han to Ch'ing." Skillfully mounted and superbly catalogued, this was, in my
opinion, the finest exhibition from the point of view of educating one's eye to con-

noisseurship in jade. The first piece, a T'ang Dynasty masterpiece, is a recumbent horse fashioned from nephrite jade containing a lot of gray and with brown markings to highlight the animal's hair. This piece gives one a completely different feeling from the late Ch'ing jadeite covered bowl. To the Western eye, the covered bowl might, at first sight, seem more attractive. The splashes of green are of a wonderful purity and luster and the piece seems to shimmer, with the green centers attracting the eye. The horse, on the other hand, looks heavy, and the luster is relatively poor. The Chinese connoisseur, however, values the horse much more than the bowl. To the Chinese eye, the T'ang nephrite horse represents a masterpiece.

The nephrite material from which this horse was fashioned came from Khotan in Turkestan (north-western China). The Chinese believed that there were three rivers in Khotan—the river of white jade, the river of green jade and the river of black jade. The pieces of jade recovered from these rivers were quite small. For at least twenty-seven centuries, from c. 1000 BC onward, miners would pan the rivers and recover jade fragments in much the same way that gold is panned. It was only at the start of the eighteenth century that the original in situ source of jade was finally located in the mountains.

Alluvial jade pieces, buffeted about as they were by water, tended to be rounded pebbles or small boulders. The skin of the material was often a different color from the inside. In nephrite the differences in color depend on the relative balance of iron and magnesium. Nephrite with a large amount of iron will be a darker shade of green; less iron would lead to a lighter, "mutton-fat" color. Jadeite, by contrast, owes its greenish color to the presence of chromium. Lavender jadeite indicates manganese content, and yellow, black or brown jadeite also occurs, these colors resulting from different admixtures of minerals.

Once the Chinese jade cutter received a pebble having a brownish skin with an off-white center, his powers of imagination and cutting skill would be stretched to the utmost. This recumbent T'ang horse is only $1^3/_8$ in. (34 mm) high and $3^3/_8$ in. (85 mm) long. The piece owes its beauty to the craftsman's inspired decision to retain the yellowish nephrite skin in such a fashion that the hair on the horse appears to be absolutely alive. The body, though heavy, also has a verisimilitude to it, with hints of brownish yellow giving it a vein-like appearance. The overall effect is one of inwardly turned tranquility was the greatest virtue and is a feature common to ceramic tomb pottery and other works of art of that dynasty.

Let us examine four different jade masterpieces to get an idea of Chinese standards for jade. The first example is a Yuan Dynasty figure, "A Boy on a Water

181 *A Mughal-style* naoratna *ring. This type of "serpentine" jade is quite common in Jaipur jewelry, even today. The nine stones are arranged in an auspicious astrological fashion.*

182 *A grey-green plaque showing animals in combat; Chinese, Western Han Dynasty (700 BC–AD 200).
Jade of this color was highly appreciated in early China.*

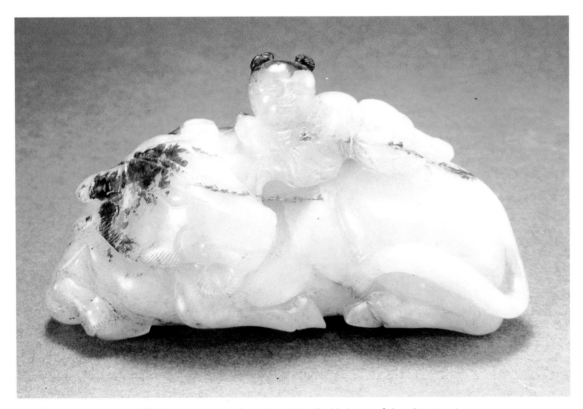

183 *"A Boy on a Water Buffalo"; Yuan Dynasty (1280–1368). The black tips of the white jade have
been utilized with consummate craftsmanship to give a playful touch to the piece, while the faint brown
line suggests a rope holding the buffalo in tow.*

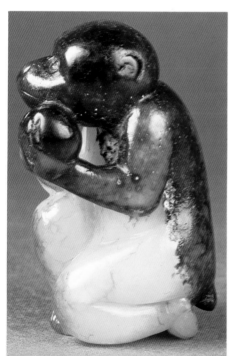

184 (ABOVE) Figure of a horse, in which all of the brownish "hair" coloring is natural. The T'ang Dynasty (960–1280) carver was able to visualize the shape of a horse while the piece of veined nephrite was still in block form.

185 (LEFT) "A Monkey with a Peach"; Ming Dynasty (1368–1644). The contrast between the brown and yellow gives this work, carved in nephrite, a sense of movement and playfulness. The luster is greater on the brown part, giving an especial vividness and movement to the head of the monkey.

186 A yellow-green mythical animal, half-tiger, half-cat; late Sung to Ming (thirteenth century or later).

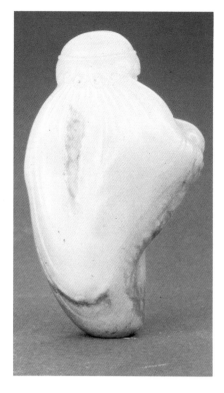

187, 188 *A T'ang tribute bearer. A foreigner (judging from his dress) is portrayed carrying a "pebble" of jade. In reality the size of jade boulders, or pebbles, would be considerably smaller than a person, and the relative size of the pebble depicted is realistic, the figure being 3¹/₄ in. (84 mm) high. Seen from the rear, the brownish rust imparts a roundness to the figure and accentuates the bowing posture of the tribute bearer. Throughout Chinese history uncarved pebbles have been considered works of art, in much the same way that uncut crystal specimens are appreciated today.*

189 (BELOW) *Ming vases. The flower arrangement on the left, which is stiff and not naturalistic, is an example of Chinese archaism, harking back to an earlier style.*

190 "Mi Fu in *Adoration, Contemplating a Rock*." In this Ming brush-pot Mi Fu is portrayed solely in white, a pure form of aestheticism; the natural world of trees and rocks takes on a brownish-green tinge. Height 4⁷/₈ in. (123 mm).

191 Pale-green jade vase or brush-pot dating from the early Ch'ing Dynasty (seventeenth century). The swirling, curving patterns convey an extraordinary representation of pine trees. Dr James Watt, in Chinese Jades from Han to Ch'ing, refers to the relationship of this design to Chinese bamboo carving.

192 *A pale-green jade thumb ring of the Ch'ing Dynasty. Thumb rings tend to be of a fairly uniform color. Often, the edges show signs of wear.*

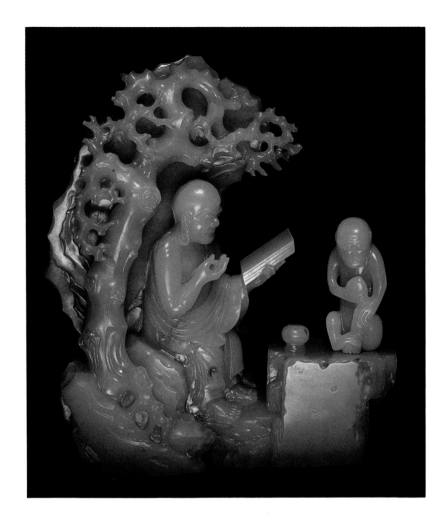

193 "Lohan in a Grotto with a Monkey." The rust-yellow markings were probably added artificially. Ch'ing Dynasty.

194 (BELOW) An eighteenth-century jade representation of a carp; Ch'ing Dynasty. All of the rust markings are part of the original, natural skin of the jade pebble.

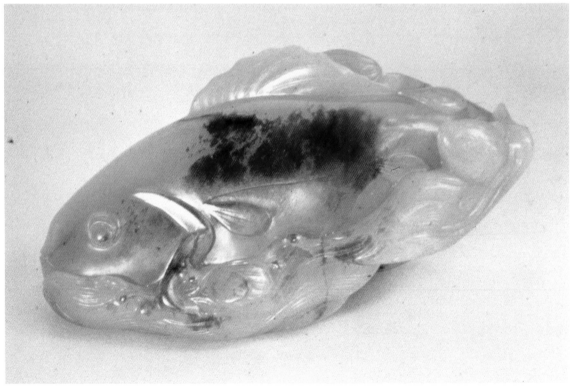

195 *A Ch'ing Dynasty pale-green jade disc 9¹/₄ in. (235 mm) in diameter; an exceptionally large piece of jade "rough" material would have been required in order to create a disc of this size.*

196 (ABOVE) *A nephrite carving of the late Chou Dynasty (fifth to third century BC). The skill of the carving and the subtlety of color shading combine to make this piece important to the Chinese eye, both from a historical and from an aesthetic point of view.*

197 *A Chinese jade marriage cup. Mounted by Fabergé in silver with stylized panther's-head motifs, the cup is set with six cabochon amethysts.*

198 A deep-green jade dish in the form of a stylized water-lily pad, encircled by a silver snake with garnet eyes. Made by Carl Gustav Armfelt for the English market, the dish is of a fine green color, sometimes called an "emerald green"; the term is, however, a misnomer because the color has no blue and is not really that of a fine emerald. To the Western eye this "emerald green" shade is more readily appreciated than the duller nephrite material.

199 (BELOW) A green jadeite bowl that is extraordinarily lustrous. The gloss is achieved both by the skill of the polisher and the inherent beauty of the jadeite material. Such luster and depth of green color are much more characteristic of jadeite than of nephrite.

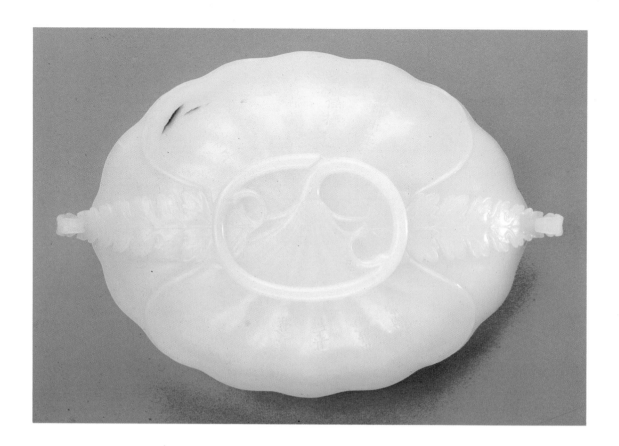

200, 201 Two views of a fabulous Mughal white jade bowl. The bowl was fashioned in India in the seventeenth century, where jade workers were even more skilled than the Chinese, a fact which was admitted in an inscription of c. 1770 engraved on the piece by a Chinese carver.

202 *A collection of Indian-fashioned jade pieces. Indian pieces often make use of delicate enamel-work that contrasts vividly with the jade.*

203, 204 Two views of a Mayan jade carving, with as yet undeciphered Mayan hieroglyphs on the bottom.

Buffalo." Here, the jade pebble from Khotan is primarily white, but with splashes of brown and blackish brown throughout the piece, in which the carver could visualize a boy sitting on a buffalo. The black-brown section of the jade was reserved for the hair, tied together in two knots on top of the boy's head in typically Chinese rural fashion. Aesthetically, this dark-brown area is balanced by similarly colored jade highlighting the outer portion of the water buffalo's horn and upper head surface. With greatly understated elegance, a thin black line is made to represent a rope connecting the boy to the water buffalo. The linkage established between the top of the boy's head, the water buffalo's head and the rope show, in a playful way, the deep connection and understanding that exist between the boy and his buffalo. In his left hand the boy holds two ears of rice. This is a pun on the word *ho*, meaning "harmony"; *ho* also means "rice." In one piece we thus have aesthetic harmony, conceptual skill and a linguistic pun. In such a union the Chinese would see genius.

An early Ming figure, "A Monkey with a Peach," is similarly a combination of the inventive use of color mixtures. The brown nephrite skin is united with the yellow body color. The brown jade has a greater lustrous surface than the yellow base, and the peach that the monkey is holding has the greatest luster of all. The monkey and the peach come part and parcel from the Indian tale of the *Ramayana*. The Chinese adopted both the story and the monkey, and introduced them into their own literature and iconography. The peach is a traditional Chinese symbol of longevity, and the monkey's remarkably persistent yet playful expression is captured in this tiny figure, only $2\frac{1}{4}$ in. (57 mm) high.

Not all jade pieces contained skin that could be used to highlight a carving, and Chinese jade carvers were not above artificially staining a piece to improve its appeal. For example, some of the yellow area seen in the crease of the "Lohan in a Grotto with a Monkey," the Lohan being one of the eighteen followers of Buddha, was created artificially. In this particular greenish-yellow jade, some natural yellow skin was present, but not enough. Thus, the eighteenth-century carver added to the coloring, and this can be identified as such with the aid of a spectroscope. The yellow is quite important to the overall aesthetic impact of the carving in that it provided a dramatic outline to the teaching Lohan. A Chinese connoisseur, however, would be able to appreciate and distinguish between the natural use of the skin and artificial staining. The latter practice was not regarded, of course, as true art.

From a simple yet powerful early Ch'ing piece (eighteenth-century), a pebble of green jade with brownish markings fashioned into a carp, we see Chinese restraint in carving. The jade boulder is only barely polished, with the outside skin revealing narrow brown veins which give the carp a highly developed aura of naturalism. This combination of colors creates the illusion of gills in the jade pebble. The pebble seems like a platonic form, more fish than fish itself.

In the Ch'ing Dynasty, after the in situ source for nephrite was found, quarrying began and larger pieces of jade became available. Skilled cutters in Shanghai, Peking and Soochow now had huge boulders with which to work. Carved jade "mountains," some of them over 8 ft (2.5 m) high, must indeed have come from truly enormous boulders. A few of these very large objects, which are now displayed in the Peking Museum, were admitted into the imperial collection.

More common than the jade mountains, of course, were jade brush-pots in the late Ch'ing period. In the magnificent Asia Society exhibition, there was shown one such pot bearing an entire scene of "Mi Fu in Adoration, Contemplating a Rock" (Mi Fu was a Ming master who had an exceptional love for the beautiful; he was a favorite subject for scroll painters as well as for jade craftsmen down the ages). The round outer surface of the brush pot matches the form of a Chinese hand-scroll, and many scenes depicted on scrolls in the Ch'ing period are mirrored in carved jade pieces. In this brush-pot the greenish portion of the skin was retained to highlight the trees, which in turn have flecks of brown to impart an even more naturalistic look to the work. Although in terms of its size, the brush-pot—measuring 4⁷/₈ in. (123 mm) in height and 4¹/₈ in. (105 mm) in diameter—is somewhat massive, there is a certain delicacy about its design. By the late Ch'ing period Chinese artisans had become exceptionally skilled in using tubular drills to go behind the surface, as it were, and were thus able to achieve a plasticity and vibrancy of form.

During the Ch'ing Dynasty, jadeite was discovered in Burma, and because of its beauty and its often intense green shade, craftsmen vied for the opportunity to work with the material. Blocks of it would be brought in from Burma and purchased by jade dealers. In China dealing in jade has always been the quintessential gambling business because jade blocks are sold "in the dark": a square block of jade will have only a sliver of the edge mawed (polished) off and therefore the balance and the shade of color in the center are an unknown quantity until the piece is actually worked on. The purchase, therefore, is very risky. At the same time, pieces of rough jade have always been extremely costly. It is not unusual today, and indeed it has been a regular practice for well over three hundred years, for several dealers to buy a piece of jade together in partnership. In the Shanghai gem markets there are stories told of immense riches made on a single piece of jade that had seemed unpromising, judging from its skin, but was later found to contain the purest shade of green inside. Of course, concomitant stories have been heard of jade dealers, wealthy for generations, who made a big mistake with a single purchase and were ruined financially.

Jadeite bowls of the nineteenth century are good examples of Chinese craftsmanship. Green jadeite need not be at its top color throughout the piece. A splash of intense color on an ordinary white background was more than sufficient for the Oriental jade connoisseur. In this respect traditional jadeite connoisseurship, at first appearing to be conservative, might seem very modern to the Western eye: just as a white Rothko canvas, having only a blotch of black on the edge, is acceptable in the context of modern painting, so too would a splotch of green suffice to please the aesthetic Chinese eye.

In the nineteenth century, Chinese craftsmen came to rely more on the material itself and on the use of tools that were increasingly technologically developed, whereas standards of workmanship started to decline. A paradox exists, therefore, in that the available material became better, the tools improved, yet the quality of the craftsmanship declined. A similar trend is noticeable even in the seventeenth century. A fabulous white jade bowl, fashioned in India in the Mughal period, was sent eventually to China where it was inscribed in Chinese, "This Hindustan bowl is as thin as paper and only the jade worker of that country is capable of making it." Indeed, there was added with true Chinese humility, "The jade worker of the interior acknowledges his inferiority." At the same time, however, the Chinese were using more sophisticated tools to cut their jade. Comparable Chinese bowls have rims with sharper edges. The Indian lapidary responsible for the Mughal piece, so thin and so translucent, achieved this result by the use of soft abrasives. Of course, the Indian method would call for months and sometimes years of work in completing a single piece. Some carved jade pieces from Mughal India found their way into the imperial collection in Peking.

Jadeite in the nineteenth and twentieth centuries became the principal high-quality carving material, although inferior pieces were also produced in exceptionally large numbers. Color standards for jadeite were similar to those established for emeralds. This similarity is not so surprising when one considers that the presence of chromium is responsible for the green in both minerals. The more yellowish the green, the less valuable the piece of jade. Occasionally, jade of a lustrous, pure shade of green would be found and the material fashioned into a man's or woman's ring.

Sometimes, exceptional pieces of jade would be matched carefully, cut in round bead forms and worn as a necklace.

Berthold Laufer, in *Jade: A Study in Chinese Archeology and Religion*, discusses the sociological aspect of jade in Chinese life. Both Mandarins and the imperial court royalty wore jade. Jade itself was "lucky" and brought further wealth. More importantly, jade personified the Confucian values of constancy, beauty and strength.

With the increased use of nephrite and jadeite in the nineteenth and twentieth centuries came the growth of jade substitutes. Chloromelanite, a variety of jadeite that is blackish green and of fairly little commercial value compared to the purer forms of jadeite and nephrite, was the workingman's jade amulet source. Tomb jade was also used. This was white nephrite that had been placed in a casket or occasionally in the body of a dead person; centuries later, the jade, which had become oxidized to a yellowish or reddish-brown color, would be exhumed. This jade was much sought after when the true yellow or brownish jadeite or nephrite could not be obtained. Bowenite, or, as it is known in China, "Hunan jade," was also used widely. This, in fact, is not jade but serpentine, and is found in many places in China and India. Serpentine can be identified readily by the connoisseur, although it is quite translucent and its color may be an intense green. Bowenite has a hardness of 5.5 and can be scratched with a sharp knife, unlike nephrite or jadeite, which are significantly harder and tougher. "Indian jade" is aventurine quartz; it was used as a jade substitute but has a luster markedly different from that of jadeite or nephrite. To the Chinese all of these other materials were regarded as of little consequence. After years of connoisseur-ship of nephrite and jadeite the Chinese are able to notice differences of color or luster immediately.

Today it is relatively simple to ascertain whether a piece is nephrite, jadeite or one of the many substitutes, by submitting it to a gemological laboratory for testing. The microscope will reveal a pitted look to jadeite and separate it from nephrite. The spectroscope will reveal characteristic spectral lines for jadeite in the blue-violet range, at 4375 angstroms. Gem-quality green jadeite, which owes its color to chromium, lacks a distinct 4375 line because the chromium produces a masking effect; in the case of nephrite, which has different characteristics, a fairly sharp line often occurs at 5090 (see Robert Webster's study *Gems: Their Sources, Descriptions, and Identification*). More difficult to test is the artificial coloring of jadeite and nephrite. As already noted, artificial coloring has been in the Chinese "bag of tricks" for at least as far back as the early Ch'ing Dynasty. Today, however, white jade can be dyed into a pleasing shade of lavender, and it is exceptionally difficult to identify this alteration, even with a spectroscope. The result is that since the use of instruments alone is inconclusive, the connoisseur's eye in judging the shade of lavender becomes an all important factor.

In the People's Republic of China today, the high standards of jade carving have been continued. In a factory in Tianjin (northern China), hundreds of craftsmen are employed. The original conception of design for a particular piece is done on paper by one worker, the design being copied from a pattern book or created as a unique piece. In practice, the vast majority of designs are copies of earlier pieces. This repetition is in the spirit of Chinese jade history, wherein archaism—the faithful copying of an earlier style, often centuries old—is much admired and respected. Once the proposed design is established, it will be passed to a master carver who will generally execute the entire piece by himself (or herself). A single jade piece can often take five or six months to complete. The material used, if it is jadeite, will have come from Burma; if it is nephrite it may still be obtained from parts of China. The Tianjin factory also buys jade substitutes and actively markets them throughout the world. An apprentice jade cutter is trained first in cutting amethyst or tiger's eye. After a number of years the worker is given the opportunity to cut jade substitutes; then, if he is exceptionally gifted as a carver, he will graduate to nephrite and perhaps, one day, work on jadeite.

Cutting jade requires an enormous amount of patience, strength and skill. After his fifties, typically, a Chinese worker will spend time acting as a teacher to a new generation of cutters who will in their turn continue the tradition. Because of the existence of a widespread market among Overseas Chinese, as well as the worldwide appreciation of Chinese jade, jade cutting has become an important industry for the country. The finest pieces, in terms of craftsmanship and material, often fetch tens of thousands of dollars.

In order to appreciate how beautiful jade can be and why it is so central in the Chinese imagination, a visit to one or more of the leading museum collections is all important. In the Smithsonian, for example, there is an exceptional group of jades, carefully catalogued and described by Paul Desautels; in particular, a vase from the Ch'ing period is an excellent example of how pure jadeite can be. The Metropolitan Museum of Art (in its H. R. Bishop collection and in its Altman collection) is exceptionally strong in its fabulous nephrite pieces. In the Victoria and Albert Museum notable archaic jades are on view, and there are other important jade collections in the Louvre, Paris, and in the Mughal collection in Bombay.

Jade is remarkable in that, while it appeals especially to the eye with its many shadings of color, and to the touch with its silky texture, it can also appeal to the ear: in an account of the Manchu Dynasty (by Princess Derling), written around the turn of the century, the sound of the tinkling of jade is described. Jade is thus particularly attractive to a connoisseur, thanks to its ability to appeal to several senses.

TEN

TURQUOISE

Blue is the color of heaven
The West is the blue world
Blue is the evening sky
Blue comes from the great turquoise mountain
—Sayings of the Zuni

"BLUE IS THE color of heaven." In all cultures from time immemorial—Far Eastern, Middle Eastern and American Indian alike—man has looked towards the heavens and been enchanted by the blue color of the sky. More than sapphire and more than lapis, turquoise has traditionally been regarded as the "sky" stone.

Turquoise having the purest and deepest shade of blue is mined in Iran. The mines there, which existed in antiquity, are situated in a remote area. West of Meshed, in northern Iran, on the southern slopes of the Kuh-e-Binalud range, in a forbidding mountainous area, lie veins of turquoise embedded in igneous rock. Dr. Eduard Gübelin has described Persian turquoise as "a secondary mineral, a product of the disintegrating, weathering, atmospheric action on rocks and adjacent ore deposits that fill fissures, cracks and cavities in rocks near the surface. It owes its formation to the dissolving and altering effects of meteoric waters which slowly break and decompose hard rocks and deposit them again later to form the sedimentary rocks."

Turquoise itself is a hydrous, extremely porous copper aluminum phosphate. If iron is present in quantity in the turquoise, the stone will be more greenish blue than pure blue. The earliest mention of turquoise is an inscription at Susa dating from the time of Darius I (fifth century BC). There are Islamic sources from the ninth and tenth centuries that speak of turquoise mines. In 1661, Jean-Baptiste Tavernier visited the gem mines and afterwards recorded his impressions in his Six Voyages to the East:

Turquoise occurs only in Persia and it is obtained in two mines. One of them, which is called the "Old Rock" is three days' journey from Meshed toward the northwest and close to a large town called Nichabourg [Neyshapur]. The other, which is called the "new" is five days' journey from the "old" mine. The stones from the "new" are of an inferior blue, tending to white, and are little esteemed. And one may purchase as many of them as one likes, at small cost. For many years the King of Persia has prohibited mining at the "Old Rock" for anyone but himself.

Examples of Islamic rings containing turquoise from both the "old" and the "new" mines have survived. Comparing the color of the turquoise in the finely worked eleventh-century Islamic ring with the color of the whiter, more greenish-blue turquoise from the twelfth-century ring, one can readily see the difference between "old" and "new" mine Persian material. The finest deep-blue turquoise would also occasionally find its way to Europe, having been exported from Persia, as is evidenced in a fourteenth-century European medieval ring.

Turquoise is not difficult to find, as it occurs either on, or close to, the surface of the earth. Cutting problems, however, are great. Turquoise, being of such a porous nature, requires special, skilled handling, and the traditional techniques of cutting turquoise, developed a thousand years ago in Persia, have not changed substantially since.

Hans E. Wulff, in his study, *Traditional Crafts of Persia*, describes the Persian gem cutter (*hakkak*), who uses:

> . . . a fiddle bow whose spindle turns the wheel and is similar to the bow drill of India. Water and Tripoli sand are used to polish turquoise. Only a master cutter will cut the *tuful*, the finest quality turquoise, whereas the lighter-color turquoise, or the turquoise with matrix spots, is left to the assistant cutters. The turquoise cutter buys the material from the mine owner. The master cutter trims the raw stones himself. The angle of trimming is critical and determines how long and how blue the turquoise will be in its polished state.

Turquoise is a national symbol of Iran, and among the country's treasures are crowns made almost entirely of pure blue, shimmering turquoise. Dr. Gübelin cites three categories of quality for Persian turquoise: first, a deep sky-blue turquoise without matrix (*angushtary*); next, stones ranging from a sky-blue shade to a greenish-blue color, with occasional veins of matrix (*barkhaneh*); and the poorest quality (*arabi*), pale gems with a lot of matrix (this type is exported to Arabia).

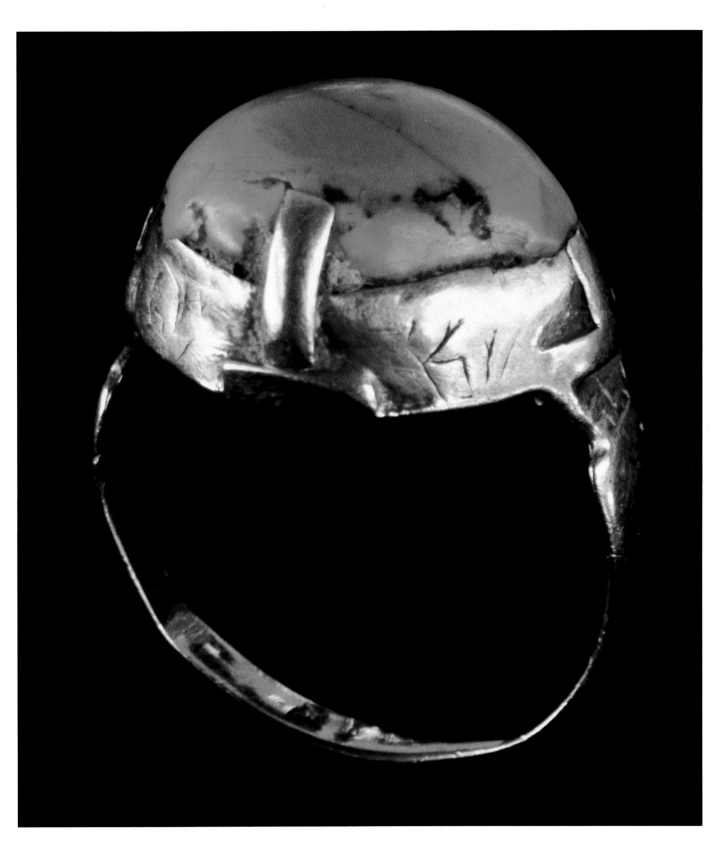

205 *An Islamic ring containing a fine-quality Persian "old mine" blue turquoise from Neyshapur. "New mine" turquoises tended to be more greenish blue.*

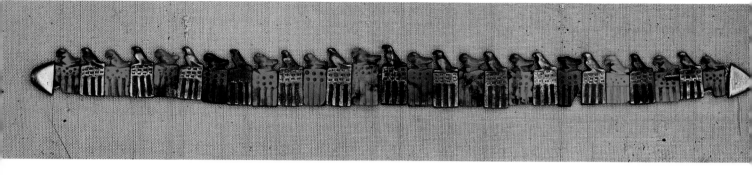

206 *A gold and turquoise bracelet consisting of alternating plaques; from the tomb of King Djer (1st Dynasty, c. 3000 BC), at Abydos. Cairo Museum.*

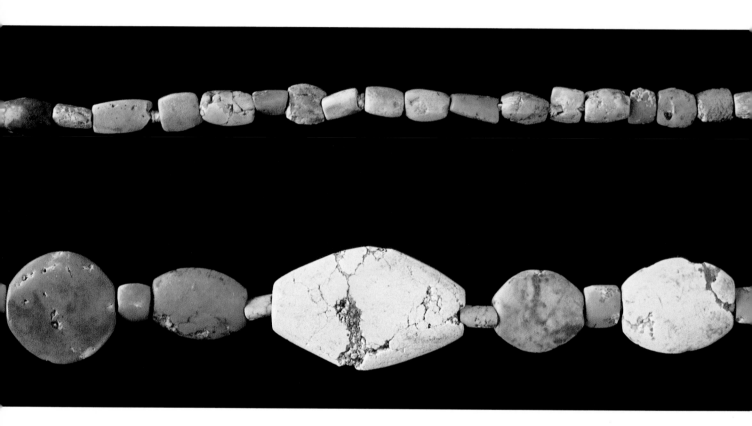

207 Strings of ancient turquoise beads; turquoise has been used for five millennia in fashioning bead necklaces. Over the centuries turquoise tends to lose its bluish color and become more greenish blue.

208 *A gold brooch by Carlo Giuliano, c. 1880, incorporating an ancient Egyptian faience scarab imitating the color of turquoise.*

209 (ABOVE) *Two medieval Islamic rings. The turquoise with a greenish cast is from the "new mine," and probably was set in the ring in either Cairo or Damascus. Turquoise was imported from Persia in the rough form and cut and set into mountings in the major Islamic jewelry centers —Cairo, Damascus (and Baghdad).*

210 *A thirteenth-century Islamic ring. This is an example of the finest shade of Persian "old mine" turquoise blue.*

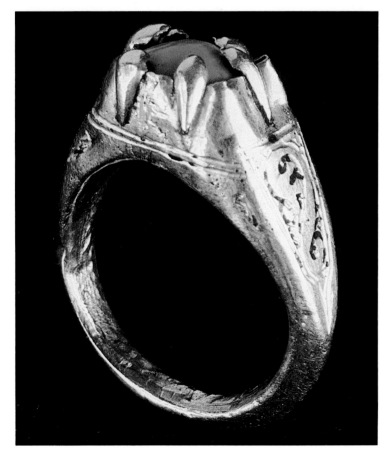

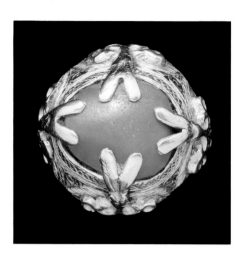
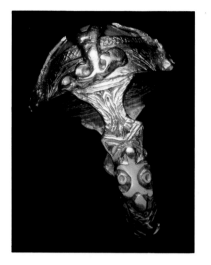

211 Three views of a medieval European turquoise (fourteenth century), bezel set with a "new mine" greenish-bluish Persian turquoise. The scalloped bezel of the ring blends sinuously into the smooth cabochon shape of the turquoise.

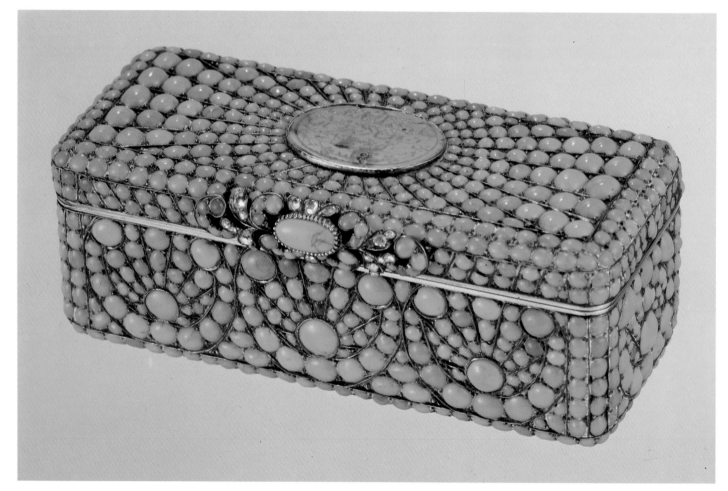

212 A superb Persian turquoise-set box inlaid with jade. Such fine matching of turquoise is seen today only in estate pieces.

213 Mask of *Tezcatlipoza* made by applying turquoise mosaic to a human skull; Mexican, believed to have formed part of a gift from the *Aztec* ruler Montezuma to the Spanish conquistador, Cortés; British Museum.

214 A gold mummy mask, repoussé, with two "eyes" of turquoise giving the mummy the power to "see" in the world to come; from Lambayeque, Peru.

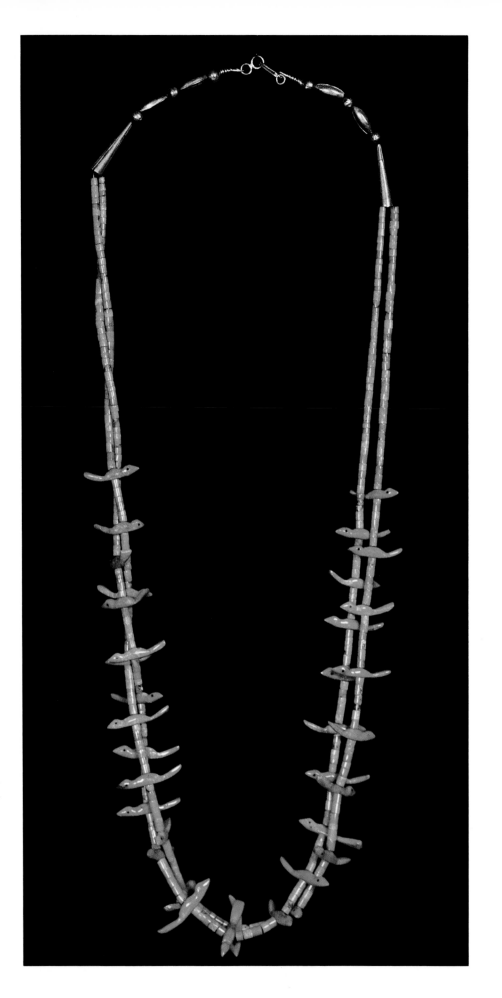

215 *A* Zuni fetish necklace. Necklaces such as this have been made in identical fashion for the last thousand years by the Zuni people. The bird motif and the color of the turquoise reinforce the traditional association between turquoise and the sky.

216 (RIGHT) Turquoise mosaic inlay work (found at Hawikuh, New Mexico). Indians have been doing such work in the American Southwest for more than a thousand years; often, the inlay is done on shell.

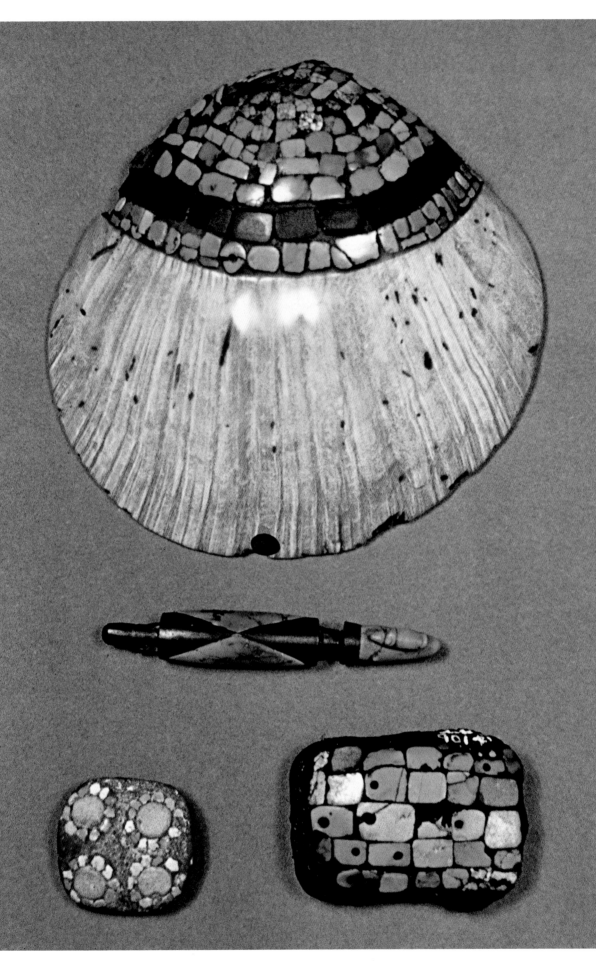

217 Shell ornament mounted in silver and inlaid with turquoise; this piece, created in the 1960s, is similar to the turquoise mosaic work found at the Hawikuh archaeological site and offers evidence of the extreme conservatism of Indian culture.

218 (BELOW) A Navajo silver and turquoise bracelet. The turquoise, with its matrix clearly evident, is at the very center of this bracelet. The bezel is built around the turquoise and not the turquoise around the bezel.

219 *A needlepoint ring recently created by a Zuni craftsman in Arizona.*

220 (BELOW) *A Zuni silver and turquoise bracelet, the style of which is much more fussy and precise than its more vigorous and spontaneous Navajo counterpart (ill. 218).*

221 *A Zuni silver "squash blossom" necklace set with turquoise. This piece from New Mexico is balanced and elegant and has even become chic in western America.*

222 *A Kingman mine nugget necklace and fetish, incorporating turquoise of an intense blue that is much prized by connoisseurs.*

223 *A selection of American Indian turquoise jeweler. The U.S. Bureau of Indian Affairs attempts to ensure that "machine work," often produced outside the United Stares, is not offered for sale spuriously marked as Indian jewelry. Genuine products are all handmade.*

224 *A turquoise brooch made in 1880. In the nineteenth century, turquoise was used widely in Europe, and especially in Russian jewelry owing to the extensive commercial contacts between Persia and Russia.*

In Tehran today, in the Bank Melli, the finest example of matched Persian turquoises can be seen. A seven-inch ceramic bowl and twelve matching drinking cups are all inlaid with sky-blue "old mine" turquoise. The pieces date from the court of Nasir ud-Din Shah Qajar (late nineteenth century), and the cups illustrate the fact that, to the Persian sensibility, a dark shade of blue, even if it contains matrix, is preferred to lighter shades. In the West, on the other hand, lighter blue shades are sought more, even if the material contains matrix.

The Persian mines are not the oldest mines in the world, however. Egyptian mines are of greater antiquity. In his *Historical Notes on Gem Mining* (1931), Sidney H. Ball claims that the first mining chief known was a captain, Haroeris, who in the twentieth century BC led an expedition for Amenemhet II into the Sinai to search for turquoise. An Egyptian document describes the torturous conditions in the Sinai: "The desert burned like summer; the mountain was on fire." Captain Haroeris kept searching the Sinai and questioning people living there, who claimed, "There is turquoise for eternity in the mountain." After three months' search Haroeris found turquoise and was able to establish Egyptian mines.

In the Sinai, nearly four thousand years ago, turquoise mines were operated with a labor force of over two thousand men. The ancient Egyptians, with their characteristic bureaucratic structures, employed military escorts, soldiers and slave laborers to extract turquoise from the ground. Examples of Egyptian turquoise have been recovered from tombs. It should be remembered that virtually the entire jewelry world of the Egyptians was centered on equipping the deceased for life after death. There were occasional rings and necklaces worn by the living, but the majority of Egyptian jewelry and almost all of their masterpieces were funerary objects, buried with the dead as an amuletic aid in the world to come.

The surviving pieces of jewelry show Egyptian turquoise to have a rather spotty greenish cast, and its quality does not bear comparison with the Persian material. Owing to the inferior quality of the available turquoise, therefore, the Egyptian master-crafts-man—whose color sense, to our modern eye, still appears superb—was desirous of "topping" turquoise. Thus, faience (fired quartz paste) came to be used, molded to provide brilliant blue surfaces. The Egyptian *baba* (faience makers) were able to create an even, rich, turquoise-blue color and use it extensively in cloisonné jewelry. The craftsmen would combine an inner case of powdered quartz with a coating of colored glaze and then coat the faience before firing with an additional layer of coloring agents. Oftentimes, the faience imitation has been so convincing as to fool art historians into believing the material to be genuine turquoise. In the long head-dress of the wife of

Tuthmosis III of Thebes, now in the Metropolitan Museum of Art, New York, one readily sees the disappointing blueness of the Egyptian turquoise as compared with the deep, "robin's-egg" blue of the faience. There can be no doubt that the practiced Egyptian eye could distinguish between the imitation, faience, and the true turquoise.

The ancient Egyptians were also able to create soda-lime silicate glass. The foundation of the glass industry can be attributed to the Egyptian jewelers' search for "imitation" turquoise. This industry can be traced back to the time of Tuthmosis III (c. 1504-1450 BC), from which period three glass jugs in various shades of blue (one, in the Metropolitan Museum, New York, being turquoise) have survived.

In some ancient cultures turquoise has always occupied a central place. In Persia, for example, it was to the ruler that the greatest pieces of turquoise went. In Egypt, Osiris, the ruler of the dead, was endowed with turquoise. Among certain American Indian tribes—the Zuni, the Navajo and the Hopi—turquoise has traditionally had special significance, being regarded as belonging to the sky gods.

At first sight, the American Southwest, the traditional homeland of the Pueblo Indians, might seem quite different from Persia and Egypt. In fact, all three areas are extremely arid and, as Joseph E. Pogue noted in his study, *Turquoise* (1915), turquoise only occurs in super-dry climates. The Indian love for turquoise pre-dates the coming of the Spaniards in the sixteenth century by many centuries. In 1897, in a remote mountainous region—the Chaco Canyon, in what is now the state of New Mexico—the Hyde Expedition discovered some fifty thousand turquoise objects. Datable pots found at the site indicate that a variety of turquoise artifacts—including beads, mosaic pendants and carved birds—were fashioned in the period 950-1150.

Turquoise was also "exported" from the American Southwest to the Indians in Central and South America. There is a fabulous Lambayeque mask inlaid with turquoise eyes characteristic of the Cerrillos mines near Santa Fe, New Mexico. Indeed, without exception, all turquoise mines ever found in the American Southwest have contained remnants, skulls or trappings of Indians who originally found and worked the mine many centuries ago. As in Persia, turquoise is found either on the surface or slightly below the surface, and only primitive mining methods need be used to recover it. The problem, however, is that turquoise tends to occur in relatively small pockets which are soon exhausted.

The Zuni believed not only that turquoise is the sky stone, but that depending on its color it is also either male or female, the perfect deep-blue turquoise being male, the greenish turquoise being female. Fetishes made of turquoise, tiny amulets worn in necklaces or treasured singly, were an important part of Zuni culture. Over the centuries the Indians mined, exported and cut turquoise. When the Spaniards came to South America and the Southwest, in the fifteenth and sixteenth centuries, traditional Indian cultures were almost totally extirpated. Gold and emeralds from South America were systematically looted and shipped in vast quantities to India as well as to Europe. Turquoise, however, was not greatly appreciated by the Spaniards. The traditional methods of utilizing turquoise—either strung on necklaces or delicately inlaid in a mosaic fashion—began to change in the late 1860s when turquoise jewelry started to appear, set in silver by Navajo and Zuni craftsmen.

How did the Navajo and Zuni master this silversmithing technique? Western Americana has it that a Navajo Indian, Atsidi Sani, learned silversmithing from a Mexican blacksmith while imprisoned at Fort Sumner in 1868. In point of fact, Kit Carson was hired by the American government in 1863 to round up members of the Navajo nation who were classified as "marauders." From 1863 to 1868 the Navajos were kept in inhuman conditions in Fort Sumner, at which point, under the terms of a treaty from Washington, they were given unpromising lands in what is now Arizona. It seems unlikely that under those conditions Atsidi Sani would have been able to learn and master the delicate art of silversmithing. In any case, either before or only shortly after their imprisonment, Navajo silversmiths had already started to produce wonderful pieces of jewelry. There is a Navajo saying, cited by Gloria Frazier, "You should not watch the silversmith when he works. If you do, things will not be done right." To the Navajo craftsman, it was not just jewelry that he was making. Rather, it was a work of personal adornment that encased fragments of the great, wide open sky.

Navajo tribal life has been the subject of intensive study. (It is said that the average Navajo family consists of a mother, a father, a brother, a sister and two anthropologists.) The Navajos have always been great travelers; they would wander from season to season, from place to place. Their jewelry is exceptionally vigorous in style. Navajo craftsmanship emphasizes the stone as opposed to the silver mounting surrounding it; the intrinsic beauty of the turquoise is emphasized and highlighted. Their work is not fussy, petite or delicate. Overall, Navajo turquoise jewelry gives a completely different feeling from that produced by the Zuni pieces. In the 1870s, after the Navajo had become more proficient in working with silver, a Navajo craftsman called Atsidi Chon traveled to the Zuni nation. In 1872 "he arrived in Zuni with one horse and left driving his horses before him." Atsidi Chon is credited with having taught the Zuni nation how to work silver.

The Zuni are quite different from the Navajo in their artistic sensibility. It is said that a Zuni craftsman can work his entire life off scraps left by a Navajo craftsman.

Meticulous, patient, sedentary and cautious, the Zuni silversmiths have created pieces of turquoise jewelry that are balanced, delicate and beautifully crafted. The Zuni will employ needlepoint engraving techniques to fashion complicated, flower-like patterns in turquoise. The Zuni craftsman first constructs the silverwork cages for the turquoise and then cuts and polishes the stones to fit into the bezels. The resulting piece will have a tailored look. To Navajo aesthetics, however, cutting the sacred turquoise to fit "mere" silver would be unthinkable.

In both cultures, Navajo and Zuni alike, the higher one's status, the finer the turquoise one would wear. A piece of turquoise jewelry is seen as the expression of the soul of the individual. When a Navajo is near to death, often in his final hours, he will bequeath his turquoise jewelry to a relative. These turquoises cannot be worn immediately by the inheritor. First, they must be "sung over," and only after four days may they be worn. At that point, an essential preliminary is that the jewelry must be washed (in soap) and, finally, the inheritor also is "sung over." Only then can the pieces be worn safely. If an Indian falls upon hard economic times, he takes his turquoise jewelry to the pawn shop, a kind of tiny grocery store with shelves in the back, in open view of the customers. The pawned items are carefully stacked up on a shelf, and a tag hanging from the jewelry clearly proclaims the name of the owner. The trader will then extend credit to the Indian to purchase coffee, bread, blankets and other essentials. Once the customer has acquired more money, he will redeem his turquoise jewelry. It is not considered bad form for the Indian to "visit" his jewelry, even when not making a purchase. The trading post serves as a kind of social center for the Navajo and Zuni.

There is no question that the Zuni and the Navajo nations feel "robbed," by the fact that today no major turquoise mine remains in their hands. The most important mines—Bisbee, Lander, Morenci and Kingman—are owned and managed by large corporate entities. Jewelry making, however, continues to be a growing southwest Indian skill. From the original polishing to the final setting, Indian craftsmen lavish great care on turquoise. The lapidary technique used is very similar to what De Sahagún, a Spaniard writing in the sixteenth century, described:

The stone that the Indians call mosaic turquoise is not very hard so that they have no need of emery to scrape, facet, smooth or polish it, for they apply it to the bamboo. Then, it receives its radiant luster and brilliance. The fine turquoise is not very hard either. They polish it likewise with fine sand and they give it a brilliant luster and radiance by the method of another polish called "the polisher of turquoise."

After fashioning the stone, the Indian craftsman carefully prepares the silver according to decades-old designs. Fetish necklaces are still common in Indian work.

What has changed is the western-American craze of non-Indians for Indian turquoise jewelry. The demand has become so strong that marginal-quality turquoise is being dyed, wax impregnated, "stabilized" and artificially treated before being sent off to factories in Massachusetts and the Far East, to be "machine worked" into Indian-style jewelry. In fact, the United States Bureau of Indian Affairs tries to ensure that only hand-made jewelry is offered for sale as "Indian jewelry." In many places, however, there has been an unwelcome cheapening of the sensitively made wares that constitute truly Indian jewelry. In the introduction to her book *American Indian Art*, Gloria Frazier writes:

> One thing may be said with emphasis for the guidance of any white man who wants to buy something really Indian—be it basket, necklace, robe or bow. If it be not well and truly made and in good taste, it is not really Indian.

All this is not to say that some Navajo will not wear blue plastic imitation beads. They will; but the beads will be regarded by the Navajo as an imitation and not something to be especially treasured.

It is not difficult to separate genuine turquoise from imitations. As a general rule, American turquoise will not be completely uniform in appearance. Turquoise occurs in a range of blue and green colors, in light and medium tones. In the case of a royal blue, the stone might be either lapis or sodalite. Turquoise imitations are most often opaque glass. Glass contains small bubbles which are visible when a 10X loupe is used. Also, glass imitations have a vitreous luster on their fracture, whereas genuine turquoise has a dull look at its fracture point. There is also pressed turquoise (Viennese turquoise), but that can be distinguished from the genuine material by placing a drop of hydrochloric acid on an inconspicuous portion of the specimen. The acid will turn the imitation a yellow-green color, but will not affect the color of genuine turquoise.

The chief problem with turquoise lies in detecting artificial stabilization and treatment. Turquoise, being extremely porous, takes dye very well. Oiling turquoise was one of the American Indians' "tricks of the trade" even before the Spaniards arrived. A Zuni tale recounts how a youth, on being given a fine turquoise to use as an offering, oiled an inferior turquoise and placed it before the gods. Heat burned the oil out and showed the stone to be of poor quality; the youth was punished by his father. The problem today is the same. Oil escapes over time. If a stone is left in a solution of carbon tetrachloride, all oil and paraffin will be removed. The stone, however, will be markedly less beautiful as a result. Indian traders use a simple test of placing several drops of hot water on the surface of turquoise. If the stone is untreated, the water will be absorbed, either slowly or quickly. This technique is not infallible as degrees of porosity in turquoise vary in stone from each mine. Administering this test requires the development of connoisseurship, therefore. While testing to separate treated from untreated turquoise is not very difficult, judging the quality of the blue in the turquoise is still a major problem.

Where is fine turquoise to be obtained today? Primarily in estate pieces. At a recent auction in Geneva, one lot consisted of a fabulous suite of "old mine" Persian turquoise, the property of Lady Deterding, wife of one of the founders of the Shell Oil Company. The necklace, earrings and ring were all perfectly matched in a robin's-egg blue, characteristic of many of the turquoises available in the 1920s. An occasional estate ring dating from before World War II will contain untreated, fine-color Persian turquoise.

American Indian turquoise, while lacking the depth of color of its Persian counterpart, still has a charm of its own because of the reverence and sensitivity that the Navajo, Zuni and Santo Domingo Indians give to their jewelry. Tibetan turquoise, also, has a large amount of matrix within it, but because of the sacred aura surrounding this Eastern people's jewelry, the turquoise can be exceptionally beautiful.

In both the American Museum of Natural History and the Museum of the American Indian, there are fine collections of nineteenth-century Indian turquoise pieces. Illustrations in the sumptuous volume *The Crown Jewels of Iran* (1968) include reproductions of finely matched turquoise cups as well as nineteenth-century Qajar turquoise pieces. The Cairo Museum has the Tutankhamun hoard—dating from the fourteenth-century BC—case after case filled with fabulous XVIIIth Dynasty earrings and necklaces containing turquoise stones (as well as thin slabs of cloisonné enamel intended to replicate turquoise). Seeing these ranges of turquoises and seeing the pieces into which they have been set makes one realize how universal has been the appeal turquoise has had among different peoples from the earliest times, symbolizing for them the sky and its ultimate mysteries.

ELEVEN

OPAL

"I found myself, one hot Wednesday, November 21, 1888, heading out to 'spot' Joe Bridle and his newly found opal mine on the burning ranges of the far Kyabra hills. And one of the whitest bushmen that ever boiled a billy went with me. The programme was to hire camels . . . strike across to Strelecki and on through Innamincka, up the Coober River to Windorah . . . to the Kyabra hills, where my meagre information fixed the man who was supposed to have made a discovery of sandstone opal . . . It seemed rather a long shot, but when I closed my eyes I could see Miss Em shake her oily ringlets and point, with a long, decisive finger, toward the North Pole. That was enough for me and I breezed off, leaving, with a pang for my young wife and a babe of six weeks."

—TULLY WOLLASTON's account of his journey, with Herb Buttfield, in western Queensland.

"NEVER NEVER" IS what the Australian aborigines call the vast uninhabited outback country. In many areas of this inhospitable terrain flies, snakes and wild kangaroos—not to mention daytime temperatures as high as 118° Fahrenheit—are common. And even the shade provided by the straggly trees that somehow manage to survive there is only sufficient to reduce the temperature by a few degrees.

It was into this forbidding terrain that Tully Wollaston, with a partner, Herbert Buttfield, set out in 1888 to find Joe Bridle who, rumor had it, had located opal. At the outset, Wollaston was not quite sure where, in fact, Bridle was, nor was he sure how to get to the Kyabra hills in western Queensland (a trek of some seven hundred miles through uncharted country). Of one thing Wollaston was certain, however: he wanted to have a chance to "spot" gem opal. In the event, Wollaston's partner perished along the way, but Wollaston did find Joe Bridle. Furthermore, the opals did exist, and indeed, they were of excellent quality. Ironically, they were of such good quality that, when Wollaston finally took a collection to Hatton Garden in London, which was the center of the world's precious-stone trade at the time, the gem dealers there had never before seen such beautiful specimens and, because of their suspicions about the stones, at first refused to purchase them.

Man's search for precious opal has continued for over two thousand years. The miraculous changes of color observed in opal have given it an irresistible allure. Opal is an amorphous, hydrous form of silica. The silica contains varying amounts of water (five to ten per cent), with the finer qualities having more. Opal is formed just below the earth's surface, generally in sedimentary deposits, in seams. Because of the relatively shallow levels of such deposits, the mining technology required is in practice quite simple; what is needed, however, is the greatest perseverance, both to find and to extract the opal-bearing boulders, or seams.

Opal was treasured in ancient Greece and Rome; their sources of supply were located in eastern Europe (present-day Czechoslovakia and Hungary). Even in the Dark Ages opal was mined and treasured, as evidenced by the survival of a splendid Merovingian ring, now in a private collection in California. This ring features a red opal set in a gold mounting with a filigree scrolling pattern about it.

Opals became a *sine qua non* of royal and aristocratic dress in Renaissance England. Queen Elizabeth I, and indeed members of the Elizabethan nobility, wore lavish parures of opal. Joan Evans recounts, in *A History of Jewelry 1100–1870*, how on New Year's Day in 1584 Sir Christopher Hatton presented a splendid opal parure to the queen. The stones came from the deposits found in volcanic lava near Czerwenitza, then in Hungary. In the splendid text to the exhibition catalogue *Princely Magnificence*, E. A. Jobbins notes that these particular opals were believed to have come from the East because they had been sold in Constantinople, but they were, in fact, of European origin. It was because of the existence of a source of supply in Hungary that opal was much sought after there and used in jewelry of the Renaissance and later periods.

In the early nineteenth century the price of opals fell by over fifty per cent, the steepest recorded price drop for any gem resulting from references in a work of literature. This dramatic change of fortune resulted from the publication in 1829 of Sir Walter Scott's late work, *Anne of Geierstein*, in which opal plays an important part.

The story in *Anne of Geierstein* concerns the fate of the Persian Shaman's daughter Hermione, who wore a wonderful gem opal:

225 *A pin featuring two separate Australian opals: the one below is from Lightning Ridge, the other from Andamooka. The pin was made in 1910 by Marcus & Company (also a wholesale importer of opal at the time).*

226, 227 *A Lightning Ridge opal necklace (front and rear views), set in Art Nouveau fashion in the United States (c. 1905).*

228 *A Hungarian opal pendant. Before the Australian opal mines were discovered, Hungary was the prime source of opal; this piece was crafted by Carlo Giuliano in the late nineteenth century.*

229 *A Victorian carved opal pansy ring (1880).*

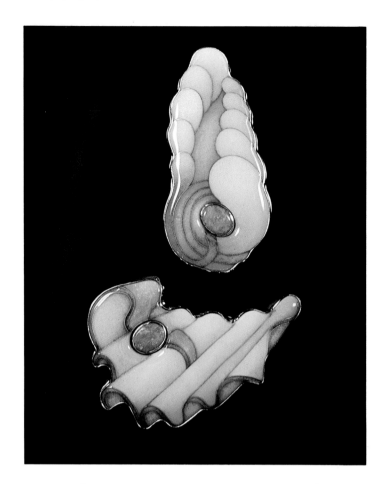

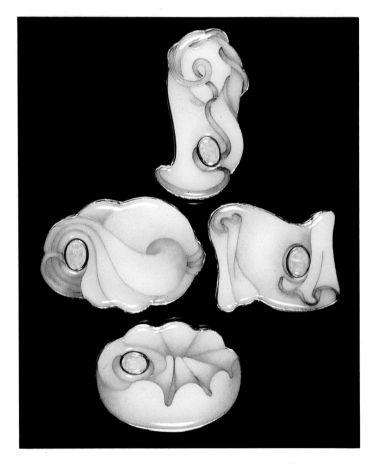

230, 231 *A selection of modern pin and pendant pieces containing cloisonné enamel, sterling silver and opal, by Connie Brauer. Modern jewelry craftsmen combine an imaginative use of gem opal with sterling silver, thereby bringing pieces such as these into an easily affordable range.*

232 (RIGHT, ABOVE) Mexican opal, or fire opal. This variety of opal frequently has an orange-reddish cast but almost no play of color; it is hence much less desirable than Australian opal.

233 (RIGHT, BELOW) A fine Lightning Ridge opal exhibiting extraordinary flashes of red, green, orange and blue. The colors seen in the first Lightning Ridge material brought to London were so extraordinary that opal dealers could not believe that the stones were genuine.

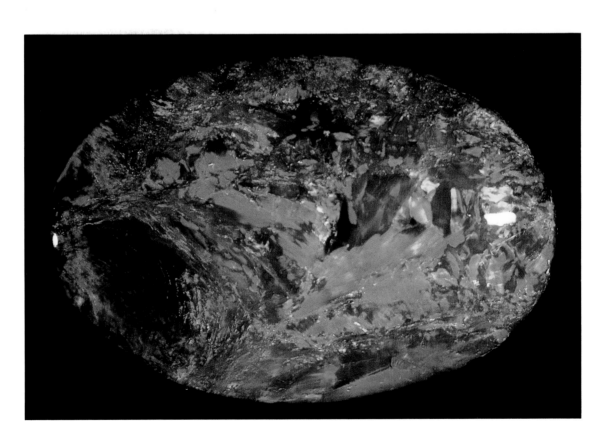

234 *An Andamooka opal, reminiscent of the palette of Monet, with soft blue and violet shading.*

235 (BELOW) *Specimens of opal material from Coober Pedy.*

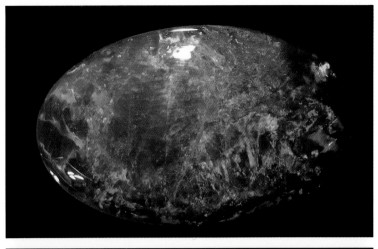

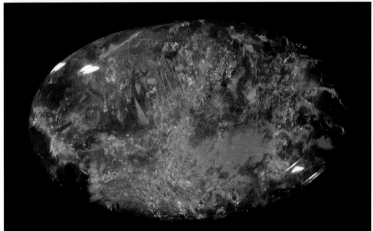

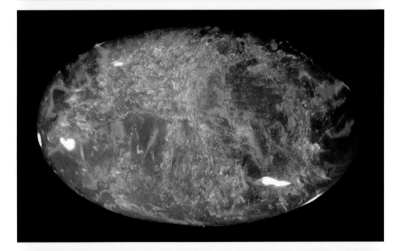

236-9 Four views of a single Lightning Ridge opal, showing the remarkable ability of opal to change its appearance, depending upon the direction of the light source. These photographs were taken with the light source rotating from the top to the side and to the bottom of the stone.

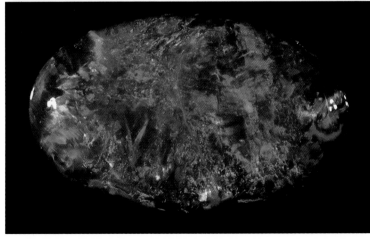

240, 241 An opal doublet; the doublet can be clearly seen when one examines its joining plane. Once this stone has been set in a "gypsy" mounting, with the girdle of the opal entirely enclosed, it becomes much more difficult to tell that it is, in fact, a doublet.

When her eyes sparkled her cheeks reddened and her whole frame became animated. It was pretended that the opal clasp amid her tresses, the ornament which she never laid aside, shot forth the little spark or tongue of flame which it always displayed with an increased vivacity. In the same manner, if in the half-darkened hall, the conversation of Hermione became unusually animated, it is believed that the jewel became brilliant and even displayed a twinkling and flashing gleam which seemed to be emitted by the gem itself and not produced in the usual manner of reflections of external light. Her maidens were also heard to surmise that when their mistress was agitated by any hasty or brief resentment (the only weakness of temper which she was sometimes observed to display), they could see dark red sparks flash from the mystical brooch as if it sympathized with the wearer's emotions. The women who attended on her toilet further reported that this gem was never removed but for a few moments when her hair was combed out and that she was unusually silent and pensive during the time it was laid aside and particularly apprehensive when any liquid was brought near it.

After Hermione became engaged and then married to a baron, she bore him a daughter. At the child's christening a mean dowager said that Hermione was a demon who was terrified of the baptismal holy waters. The baron foolishly and impatiently offered the holy water to his lady. A drop of it touched the opal.

The opal shot out a brilliant spark like a falling star and became, the instant afterward, lightless and colorless as a common pebble, while the beautiful baroness sank to the floor of the chapel with a deep sigh of pain.

Lady Hermione was carried to her bedchamber and spoke with the baron for an hour, after which he left and prayed in the chapel. A doctor was then sent for to tend Lady Hermione.

When upon opening the door of the chamber in which the baroness had been deposited little more than two hours before, no traces of her could be discovered, unless that there was about a handful of light gray ashes like such as might have been produced by burning fine paper, found on the bed where she had been laid.

What had proved a tragic day for the fictional baron created a difficult situation for the opal dealers in Europe. Such was the popularity of Scott's novels that there was a widespread reaction, and it was only in the late nineteenth century that opals were again restored to favor. Extraordinary finds of opal had recently been made at White Cliffs and Lightning Ridge, both in New South Wales, Australia. The Lightning Ridge opals, especially, with their glorious dark background and their brilliant display of colors, opened up a range of design possibilities for opal jewelry that had not existed for the Hungarian varieties. Once the Lightning Ridge and White Cliffs sources started to become exhausted, enterprising miners began digging below the arid surface in South Australia. Precious opals were discovered in 1915 at Coober Pedy (the name for the mine is derived from the Aboriginal phrase "Kupa piti," meaning "white man under ground," used to describe the dugouts to which the miners retired to escape from the oppressive heat), and at Andamooka (discovered in 1930). On a visit to Adelaide in 1954, Queen Elizabeth II was presented with a splendid opal from Andamooka. Today, South Australian sources supply about eighty per cent of the world's output of precious opal, including some fine-quality material (black and white) from the more recent mine at Mintabie (first discovered in 1931, but not commercially exploited until 1976), some 200 miles north-west of Coober Pedy.

Connoisseurship in judging the quality of opal depends upon the recognition of three things: the background color of the stone, the pattern in which the opal's color is distributed, and the character of the color. There are four basic types of opal: black opal, white opal, transparent opal and common opal. In the wholesale trade black opal is often called "Australian opal." In fact, Australian black opal tends to come from Lightning Ridge. The blackness of the background makes this type of opal a very dramatic and appealing gem. White opal is often termed "Hungarian opal" by traders, but this is a misnomer for there is today a great deal of Australian opal with light backgrounds, coming from the Coober Pedy mine as well as from the Andamooka mine. Transparent opals tend to be either fire opals or water opals, and are often called "Mexican opals." While they have pleasing colors, the degree of their iridescence is significantly less, and they are less sought after by connoisseurs. Often, Mexican opals, especially the fire kind, are mistaken for topaz or smoky quartz. The fourth type, common opal, has no play of color at all and has very little commercial value. The beauty of gem black opal and gem white opal depends upon the pattern and on the depth of the play of color.

The scientific reason for opals having their play of colors has been much disputed. Recent theories rely on electron microscope analyses of the structure of opal molecules. In point of fact, opals tend to have different "stacks" of silica molecules (which, when seen under magnification, resemble rows of tennis balls arranged in various heights). The stacks vary with the amount of water present in an opal, as well as with the silica itself. The light hits each of these stacks and, by hitting the molecules at the varying levels, is reflected in different patterns. The resulting iridescence is produced in a manner identical to that which causes a water puddle to glisten in the sunlight.

The most desirable iridescent pattern is the "harlequin." Sometimes, precious opal will show a mosaic-like chromatic pattern in patches of equal size. These patches can be angular, square or round, and the spangled appearance that they give came to be known as harlequin (from the traditional costume of the Commedia dell'Arte character). The most desirable colors for black opal, in order of preference, are red, violet, orange, yellow, green and blue. A black opal in a harlequin pattern with intense reds, violets and oranges is considered the most sought-after type. Sometimes, the pattern within a black or white opal will have a rolling or flash-like quality. Flash opals are difficult to illustrate in photographs because of the "frozen" quality of a single image, but when seen directly, the effect is quite extraordinary. Sometimes, the flash opal will have an elongated, streaked effect and will be called a "flame opal." When a flame opal is turned, its changing colors bear a remarkable resemblance to the dancing flames in a log fire. Slightly less sought after than the harlequin, flash and flame patterns is the pinfire variety, where the colors seem localized. By way of analogy, the effect of the pointillist technique used in Impressionist paintings, for example Seurat's masterpiece *Sunday Afternoon on the Island of La Grande Jatte*, is quite similar to the pinfire opal. In the white Australian opals from Andamooka and Coober Pedy, although the background is not as dramatic as that of the black opals, flash patterns can be unusually beautiful. The magnificent play of red, violet and orange among the sea of blue and green produces an effect that is very reminiscent of Claude Monet's studies of water-lilies.

An important though less gem-like opal is the Mexican fire opal. Generally, it is of a brownish or orange color, without the marked iridescence of the Australian opals. Mexican opals are more transparent and can be fairly lively when set. They are used widely in commercial jewelry—rings, brooches and pins. Occasionally, they are mistaken for topazes because of the similar color. When Mexican opal is colorless it is called "water opal." Lacking the color of fire opal and the iridescence of precious opal, water opal is not much sought after by connoisseurs.

Given the difficulty of finding opal and the rarity of gem opal, it is not surprising that imitations and synthetics should abound. The most common substitute would be an opal doublet. This is a thin slab, generally of black opal, mounted on a white base. The base can be either a poor-quality opal or another gem material, or even glass or plastic. When such a doublet is mounted in a "gypsy" setting, with a completely enclosed girdle, identification is very difficult. When loose, however, the joining plane of the doublet, where the cement fixes the two surfaces, is clearly discernible to a trained eye. Where an opal is set in a ring with an open back (under-bezel), if a play of color can be observed both on the top of the bezel and on the under-bezel, one can be certain that the opal is all of a piece and is not a doublet.

An opal triplet is an opal doublet that has been, in turn, cemented to a rock crystal stone to give the opal greater durability; such triplets are very common in the Australian jewelry world. As in the case of doublets, they can be distinguished from gem opal if the joining plane can be seen. Opal doublets and triplets have little commercial value, as compared to complete, whole opals.

Often, today, genuine opal, especially the black variety, is treated either with heat or by the addition of sugar or other materials, to improve its color. With the aid of a magnifying glass one can often detect black spots on the surface of the opal, indicating that it has been subjected to such artificial treatment. Glass is frequently used to imitate opal, but opal's refractive index is considerably lower and provides an easy method of distinguishing the genuine stone from glass.

In the 1970s Pierre Gilson, a ceramicist in France, experimented widely and successfully with the effects of heat on various materials and was able to create, among other things, an extraordinary synthetic opal. Even very experienced wholesale dealers were taken in, but Gilson has always maintained that the object was not to fool the gem connoisseur, merely to create an affordable piece of "opal" jewelry. With the aid of a spectroscope and magnification, synthetic opal can be readily separated from the genuine gem counterpart.

One plausible reason for the belief that opal could bring a change of fortune to its owner is to be found in the stone's fragility. More than any other precious gem, opal is remarkably susceptible to changes in its water content or in temperature. Very often, fine cracks will appear on the surface. This "checking" or crazing greatly interferes with the play of color and, of course, the value of the opal. Opal should be cleaned with a dry cloth, and should be kept away from perfumes and all strong chemicals and detergents.

Opal, more than any other gem, is best appreciated when worn. Then, the movement of the stone gives a play of color that cannot be seen or appreciated fully when the opal is static or imprisoned within a "museum case." Notwithstanding this drawback, the American Museum of Natural History houses an extraordinary and indeed beautiful collection of opals, in both cut and uncut states. The Smithsonian Institution has a splendid specimen collection of opals from sources the world over. In the Roebling Gifts there are a 355-carat black Nevada opal, a 155-carat Australian white opal and a 55-carat colorless Mexican opal, with fire. The 27-carat Lightning Ridge opal, with a splendid display of red, green, yellow and blue, is an absolute gem. Similarly, the 30-carat deep orange-brown fire opal in this collection was expertly cut by John Sinkankis, the noted mineralogist, author and lapidary, to display its qualities of liveliness and a fine luster to full advantage.

As is to be expected, some of the most extraordinary specimen opals have remained in private collections in Australia. The Butterfly, or Red Admiral, stone was cut in a butterfly heart-shaped form and is considered by many to be the best-known example of red, blue and green flame opal. Percy Marks, in Sydney, has an outstanding collection of Lightning Ridge and other Australian-location opals.

The name opal is derived from the Greek *opallios*, meaning "change of color." The Indonesian name for it is based on the Sanskrit *maya*, or "illusion," and the Javanese *kali*, "river"; hence the Indonesian term *kalimaya*, "river of illusion." In both the West and the East, opal—with its fiery color and its wondrous ability to change its appearance when seen from different angles—provides the gem connoisseur with an excellent example of beauty and aesthetic movement in nature.

TWELVE

GARNET

In sorrow of soul they laid on the pyre
Their mighty leader, their well-loved lord.
The warriors kindled the bale on the barrow,
Wakened the greatest of funeral fires.
Dark o'er the blaze the wood-smoke mounted;
The winds were still, and the sound of weeping
Rose with the roar of the surging flame
Till the heat of the fire had broken the body.
With hearts that were heavy they chanted their sorrow,
Singing a dirge for the death of their lord;
. . .

The men of the Weder folk fashioned a mound
Broad and high on the brow of the cliff,
Seen from afar by seafaring men.
Ten days they worked on the warrior's barrow
Inclosing the ash of the funeral flame
With a wall as worthy as wisdom could shape.
They bore to the barrow the rings and the gems,
Collars, brooches and necklaces,
The wealth of the hoard the heroes had plundered.
The olden treasure they gave to the earth,
The gold to the ground, where it still remains
As useless to man as it was of yore.

—Beowulf's funeral, c. AD 700;
from *Beowulf* (trans. Charles Kennedy)

THE COLOR RED lay at the heart of the world view of the migrating hordes that swept across Europe after the decline of the Roman Empire. What the Avars, the Huns, the Franks and the Merovingians had in common was their wandering across central Asia and Europe, fighting to capture lands for themselves. Although warlike peoples, their art and, especially, their jewelry are of a high standard. Their martial spirit found quintessential expression in the color fiery, blood-red garnet jewelry. In order to obtain an idea of the splendor

223

of surviving jewelry of the Migration period, and of the importance of garnet in that jewelry, one need only visit the British Museum, where the magnificent treasure recovered from the Sutton Hoo ship burial is displayed. Here, one can see a complete collection of grave goods associated with the burial of an important (but unidentified) warrior in the seventh century. The objects include a gold purse-lid, splendid shoulder-clasps and wonderful rectangular buckles, their gleaming garnets as bright red as ever. How were these stones fashioned, and from where did they come?

The garnets in post-Roman times tended to be of the rich, deep-red pyrope variety, probably from mines in what is now Czechoslovakia. Garnet is the name given to a group of minerals having a similar chemical composition and a similar crystal formation. Today, garnets tend to be divided along color lines. Pyrope garnet tends toward a ruby-red color, spessartite toward a yellowish- or brownish-red, almandine toward a violet-red, while demantoid is a green variety. Stones of the garnet family, crystallizing as they do in a cubic system, can be separated into parallel slivers by careful cleaving. The Migration jewelers were able to take chunks of rhombic garnet and strike them at the cleavage plane. The resulting slivers could be carefully fixed onto cement, which in turn, would be placed in tiny cloisons (gold or metal raised wire boundaries) which were set on top of a metal base, generally also of gold. The gold base was chisel-cut. After the garnet was placed in the cloison, one could readily see how the carefully tooled, chisel-cut background served to enhance the brilliance of the stone's color. Modern scholars believe that the Sutton Hoo pieces owe their regularity and superb perfection to the use of a punch chisel that repetitively stamped out the backings of the cloisons. In addition, the greatest possible care was taken in the cleaving and color matching of the garnet slivers, resulting in an overall regularity and perfection of craftsmanship unequalled in jewelry making before or since. While the identity of the noble person associated with Sutton Hoo is unknown, there is no question but that he was an important figure in the Merovingian period.

The very use of garnet suggests the importance of Sutton Hoo, for in the hundreds of European burial sites of the period that have been excavated, common people were never buried with either red beads or red earrings. According to Gyula Laszlo, a professor of archaeology at Budapest University, the color red and, of course, garnet jewelry were clearly fit only for nobles and kings. It is to be recalled that the faceting of colored stones and the cutting of stones other than as cabochons became technologically feasible only from the fifteenth century on. Thus, in the earlier period, even if a ruby were found, garnet would offer a redder color because

242 *A 22-carat gold ring set with a classical Greek heart-shaped glistening garnet.*

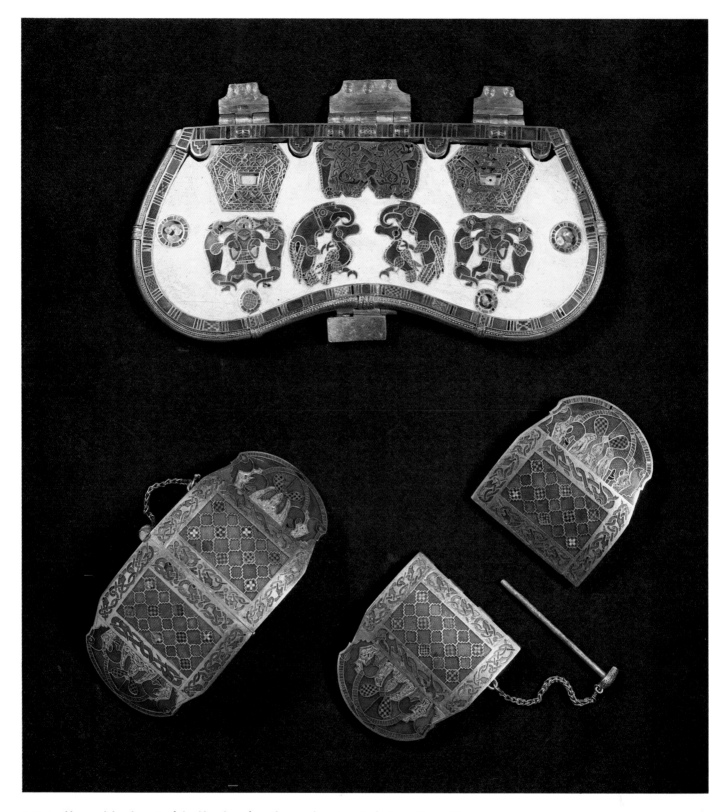

243 *A gold purse-lid and a pair of shoulder-clasps from the seventh-century Anglo-Saxon Sutton Hoo ship burial, all containing cloisonné garnet and millefiori glass. The interlocking motifs of the purse-lid bear witness to the connection between Migration jewelry and its central Asian antecedents, while in the shoulder-clasps the garnets are meticulously mounted on an engraved gold background which gives the stones additional "life." British Museum.*

244 (ABOVE, LEFT) *The Kingston Brooch, found at Kingston Down, in Kent, is one of the finest pieces of Anglo-Saxon polychrome jewelry, dating from the period c. 550–700. The gold brooch features cloisonné garnet, lapis lazuli and cuttle-fish bone.*

245 (ABOVE, RIGHT) *Another seventh-century jeweled piece from the Sutton Hoo burial exhibits a degree of elegance and precision which completely belies the description "barbarian," often applied to jewelry of this period.*

246 *A detail of one of the shoulder-clasps from the Sutton Hoo burial (cf. ill. 243).*

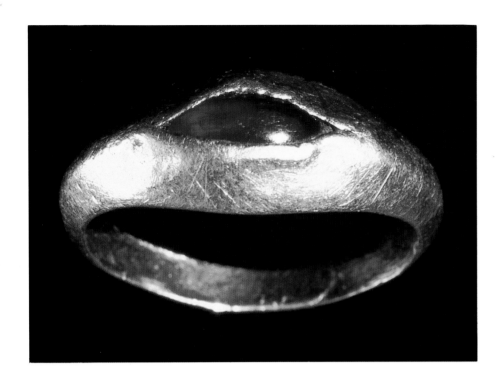

247 *A Roman garnet ring in the shape of an eye;
the eye was intended as a talisman to protect the
wearer.*

248, 249 (BELOW) *Two views of an English
medieval garnet ring set in a "pie-dish" bezel. This
stone, which originated in Ceylon, proves that in
medieval times trade routes did exist between
Ceylon and England.*

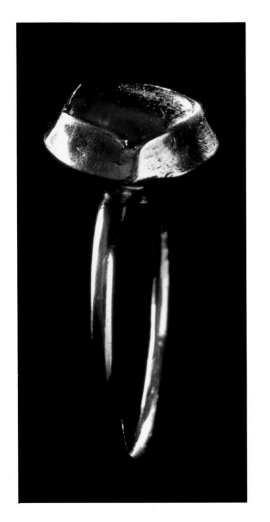

250 The eagle-brooch is characteristic of the art of the early Germanic peoples. These two examples, from Estremadura in Spain, are among the finest surviving specimens; the body is circular, with head, wings and tail added. The red color is produced by garnets, all the blue and green inlays are of glass, while the white "eye-balls" are opals and the central stones quartz.

251 (BELOW) Examples of Sarmatian gold earrings with inset garnets, from sites in the Crimea, c. fourth century.

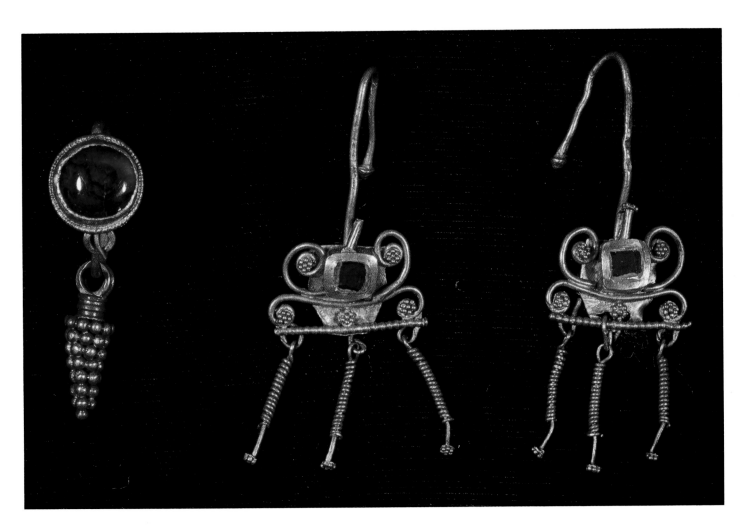

252 *A Victorian carbuncle garnet. This piece would have been prohibitively expensive had a ruby of the same size been used.*

253 *A Renaissance garnet ring, c. 1620, with perfectly matched, pyramid-cut garnets. The shape of the garnets is meant to match a natural uncut octahedral diamond crystal.*

254 (BELOW) *A massive Victorian garnet bracelet.*

255 Demantoid garnet's extraordinary brilliance highlighted in two zoomorphic pins. Having a much greater refractive index than emerald, the green garnet of the frog gives it a more vivid and lifelike appearance than it would have had if the piece had been set with emeralds. Similarly, the garnet "eyes" of the butterfly's wings are more lively than the two emeralds set in gold wire. The frog is Russian, late nineteenth century, and the butterfly, French, c. 1910.

256 Tsavorite garnet rings. Tsavorite is a green grossular garnet with a high luster and refractive index. Often costing a quarter of the price of emerald (or less), it has been promoted successfully by Tiffany's and other fine jewelry stores as a more easily affordable green stone. These rings are part of Tiffany's collection of tsavorite and diamond pieces.

of the sliver technique. Hence the Romans mined garnet extensively in Europe and even imported supplies from as far away as India.

Garnets are most sensibly categorized by color, that is, red, brownish red, purplish red, green and other colors, since from a mineralogical point of view, the stones of each color really constitute a group. However, garnets are sub-divided by the admixture of other minerals. For example, grossular is a calcium garnet. Its orange variety is called hessonite. Pyrope garnet has manganese in it and is a deep red color. Spessartine is also a manganese garnet and it is orange or reddish, or yellowish orange. Almandite has a great deal of iron, and therefore is a very red color. Andradite garnet has calcium and iron in it, and can be different colors. When it is green, it is called demantoid. Garnet specimens, in fact, should in many cases be classified as a combination of two varieties. Seen under a microscope, almandine garnet has a characteristic cross-hatched silk pattern and also zircon crystals. Hessonite often displays a rolling, liquid-like, heat-wave effect; this is because the color is unevenly distributed in a wave-length pattern. Pyrope garnet tends to have long needle-like crystals. Green demantoid garnet reveals a rather striking "horsetail" inclusion which marks it immediately as genuine and demantoid. The refractive index of both demantoid garnet and that of grossular garnet is much higher than the refractive index of emerald, so that distinguishing them should not present a problem. In the case of red garnet, it can be distinguished on a microscope-inclusion basis—the silk of a ruby occurs at angle of 60° and not 110° as it does in garnet. There is a difference, also, in the refractive index of ruby and garnet. Finally, ruby can be distinguished from garnet by its characteristic very sharp spectral lines, occurring somewhere between 6,500 and 7,000 angstroms in a spectroscopic reading.

Red garnet has been in demand for jewelry since antiquity. The name itself comes from the Latin *granatum*, pomegranate, due to the resemblance of the color of its seeds of that of garnet. In the Bible, the word "carbuncle" (from the Latin word meaning "little coal") refers to red stones of whatever type. The Romans used garnet along with ruby and glass, in cabochon form, in rings and in other jewelry. It is not clear at all whether Roman jewelers were able to distinguish garnet from ruby, but the Roman lapidary who cut the garnet would have been able to tell the difference from the varying hardnesses of garnet, ruby and, of course, glass. One of the earliest extant price lists of gems comes from an eleventh-century jeweler in Cairo. In this list the term "balas ruby" is used, but this refers not to a ruby or a garnet but to a spinel. Red stones, until the early Renaissance period, were often generally described as "ruby" even though, in fact, they might have been garnet (pyrope or almandine), spinel or even glass.

During the Renaissance the redness of garnet lost the martial symbolism associated with it in Roman and Migration times. It assumed, instead, a religious significance associated with the Passion of Christ and the Crucifixion. Frequently, garnets would be arranged in a cruciform setting. Garnets tended to be displayed in a table-cut fashion, not because of the stone's crystal shape, but rather in imitation of the table-cut style used for diamonds. (Diamond crystals, given their great hardness, could not be faceted easily, but could be "worn down," so that the point of the diamond would be flattened to produce a table-cut shape.) Renaissance garnets of the pyrope variety were termed "Bohemian rubies" in the jewelers' manuals of the time; these stones would be obtained by surface mining. Almandine stones, however, would come from as far away as Ceylon. Anna Somers-Cocks, of the Victoria and Albert Museum, describes a hessonite garnet that was cut and placed in a pendant in the seventeenth century. The back of the setting is open so that the garnet might rest on the skin of the wearer. According to Joan Evans, who in fact gave that piece to the Museum, garnets in Renaissance times were said to relieve fever.

In Victorian times there was a tremendous explosion of wealth in certain sectors of British society, due not only to the acquisition of colonies throughout the world but also to technological advances achieved by British inventors in industry. Not only did the aristocracy expand its patronage of gem-quality rubies, sapphires and emeralds, but the middle class also increased its appetite for gemstones. Garnets, with their deep-red color, became an affordable ruby-substitute. Brooches set in bow forms reminiscent of the aristocratic bow brooches, kidney-shaped pins and quite large carbuncle (cabochon cut) garnet bracelets were created by fashionable British jewelers.

Although to the layman, the mention of garnet immediately brings to mind reddish stones, probably massed in Victorian jewelry, the important exception is green demantoid garnet. The term demantoid is derived from the Dutch *demant*, or "diamond." The stone is a variety of the andradite group (named after the Portuguese mineralogist, D'Andrada), and was first found only in the last century in Russia. The distinctive color of demantoid garnet is produced by the presence of chromium, and ranges from pure green to yellowish green. At its finest it rivals emerald in its purity of green, and, because of its great brilliance, it is considered a most precious gem. Sizes above one carat are exceedingly rare, however.

Imaginative European designers, especially Russians, would fashion pins in the shape of animals, using demantoid garnets to highlight the skeletal outline. An exquisite example of this technique, crafted in the late nineteenth century, is a frog having its entire back covered in ten-point garnets. The same piece, if set with emeralds, would look much less "real" because of the emerald's lesser brilliance.

Another type of green garnet is the green grossular variety. In 1969 Henry B. Platt, then president of Tiffany's, was shown a clear green grossular garnet while visiting Africa. The newly mined stone tended toward a yellowish green, and was very brilliant. Platt had previously launched and named "tanzanite," the blue zoisite, that had been discovered in Tanzania two years before.

Tanzanite had proved a remarkable commercial success, since it filled a price void for blue stones, finding a market among the many people who wanted a blue stone but couldn't quite afford sapphire. Platt's sensitivity to the public's desire for an emerald-like stone at a more affordable price level led to great excitement at Tiffany's. The problem was that Tanzanian officials had already contracted for the production of grossularite where it was first seen by Platt. Tiffany's did not want to buy the gems third- and fourth-hand, so they decided to take an even greater gamble—to discover and develop deposits on their own.

Platt prudently decided to get in touch with the well-known authority, Campbell Bridges. In the 1974 summer issue of *Gems and Gemology*, Bridges describes the mineralogical formulation of the grossular deposit. Basically, Bridges figured out that the known Tanzanian sedimentary deposit must extend south-eastward into Kenya, and outcroppings of the deposit were duly found near Tsavo National Park. The material occurred not only in gem quality but in large enough quantities to encourage Tiffany's to promote the gemstone. Although "tsavorite," as Platt decided to call it, had a less intense, less saturated, green color than tanzanite, it nevertheless found a place in the commercial world. Selling for less than a quarter of the price of emerald, the stone adorns many modern jeweled settings.

There are other green garnets such as uvarovite, pale greenish in color, but they are so rare as to be of interest primarily to collectors, not jewelers. Paradoxically, if a stone becomes virtually unobtainable, it cannot be considered a gem, as, in fact, there is not enough to create jewelry or stimulate public demand.

Garnet, through the centuries, has had the dual advantage of a sought-after color and a relative lack of rarity. From the Avars to avaricious Victorians, jewelers have set garnets in all manner of brooches, rings, helmets, necklaces and bracelets. In its green variety, the most elegant of jewelers, Fabergé and Tiffany, have capitalized on the brilliance of demantoid and on the luster and delicacy of tsavorite, respectively. Thus, garnet in its various forms continues to be both versatile and important as a gem, with the added advantage of being less costly than ruby or emerald.

DOCUMENTARY
ILLUSTRATIONS

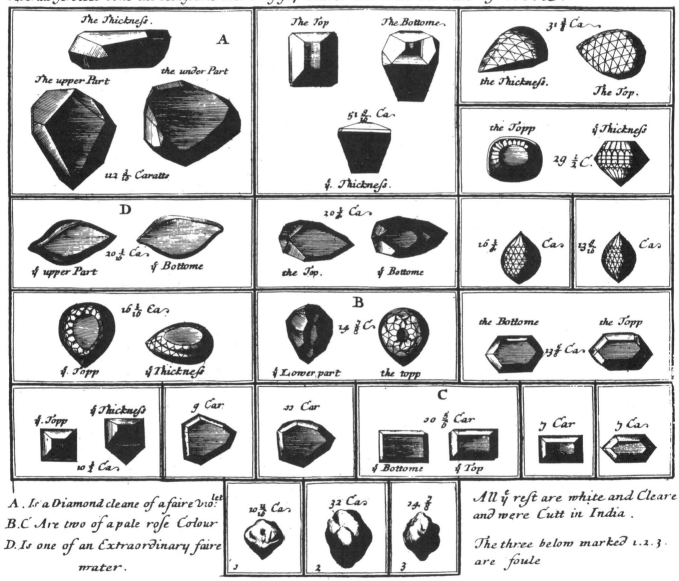

Page 149 A Representation of 24 y fairest Diamonds Chosen out among all those which   Travels in India.
Monsieur Tavernier sold to y King at his last return from the Indies, upon which Consideration, and for
severall services done the Kingdome His Majesty honored him with the Title of Noble.

A. Is a Diamond cleane of a faire violet.
B.C Are two of a pale rose Colour
D. Is one of an Extraordinary faire
water.

All y rest are white and Cleare
and were Cutt in India.

The three below marked 1.2.3.
are foule

A page of drawings by Jean Baptiste Tavernier, showing a selection of diamonds sold by him to Louis
XIV of France.

GIA
GEM TRADE LABORATORY

New York Headquarters
580 Fifth Avenue | New York, NY 10036-4794
T: 212-221-5858 | F: 212-575-3095

Carlsbad
5355 Armada Drive | Carlsbad, CA 92008-4699
T: 760-603-4500 | F: 760-603-1814

DIAMOND GRADING REPORT

GIA REPORT 12284241

October 30, 2002

Shape and Cutting Style	EMERALD CUT
Measurements	8.98 x 7.43 x 4.29 mm
Weight	2.40 carat
Proportions	
Depth	57.7 %
Table	69 %
Girdle	EXTREMELY THIN TO MEDIUM
Culet	SMALL
Finish	
Polish	GOOD
Symmetry	GOOD
Clarity Grade	VS2
Color Grade	G
Fluorescence	NONE

Comments:
NONE

111347201

This Report is not a guarantee, valuation or appraisal. This Report contains only the characteristics of the diamond described herein after it has been graded, tested, examined and analyzed by GIA Gem Trade Laboratory under 10X magnification, and/or has been inscribed, using the techniques and equipment available to GIA Gem Trade Laboratory at the time of the examination and/or at the time of being inscribed, including fully corrected triplet loupe and binocular microscope, master color comparison diamonds, standardized viewing environment and light source, electronic carat balance, synthetic diamond screening device, high intensity short wave fluorescence imaging system, short wave ultraviolet transmission detection system, optical measuring device, micro laser inscribing device, ProportionScope®, ultraviolet lamps, millimeter gauge, and ancillary instruments as necessary. Red symbols denote internal characteristics (inclusions). Green or black symbols denote external characteristics (blemishes). Diagram is an approximate representation of the diamond, and symbols shown indicate type, position, and approximate size of clarity characteristics. All clarity characteristics may not be shown. Details of finish are not shown. The recipient of this Report may wish to consult a credentialed Jeweler or Gemologist about the importance and interrelationship of cut, color, clarity and carat weight.

GIA CLARITY SCALE

FLAWLESS
INTERNALLY FLAWLESS
VVS₁
VVS₂
VS₁
VS₂
SI₁
SI₂
I₁
I₂
I₃

VERY VERY SLIGHTLY INCLUDED
VERY SLIGHTLY INCLUDED
SLIGHTLY INCLUDED
INCLUDED

GIA COLOR SCALE

D
E
F
G
H
I
J
K
L
M
N
O
P
Q
R
S
T
U
V
W
X
Y
Z

COLORLESS
NEAR COLORLESS
FAINT
VERY LIGHT
LIGHT

KEY TO SYMBOLS
Feather
Cloud
Pinpoint

IMPORTANT DOCUMENT, STORE SAFELY

NOTICE: IMPORTANT LIMITATIONS ON BACK
COPYRIGHT ©2000 GEMOLOGICAL INSTITUTE OF AMERICA, INC.

A diamond certificate issued by the Gemological Institute of America. Diamond certificates are "all important" in giving a clear profile of a diamond: size, cut proportions, whiteness of color wwith D, E, F being colorless as well as degree of fluorescence, graining, etc.

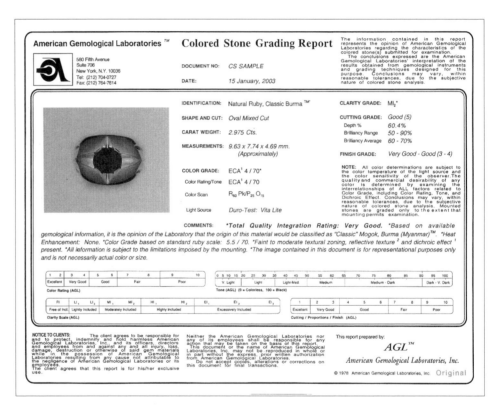

Colored stone certificated (ruby, sapphires, emeralds) state the mining origin of the gem: Burma, Ceylon, etc. A color analysis is also given. Finally, any enhancement by heat or oiling is stated. There are also certificates of dates of creation for antique jewelry—for example, Cartier will issue a certificate stating the date the piece was created and also state which branch (Paris, London, or New York) crafted the piece.

American Gemological Laboratories ™   **Colored Stone Grading Report**

580 Fifth Avenue
Suite 706
New York, N.Y. 10036
Tel: (212) 704-0727
Fax: (212) 764-7614

The information contained in this report represents the opinion of American Gemological Laboratories regarding the characteristics of the colored stone(s) submitted for examination.
The conclusions expressed are the American Gemological Laboratories' interpretation of the results obtained from gemological instruments and grading techniques designed for this purpose. Conclusions may vary, within reasonable tolerances, due to the subjective nature of colored stone analysis.

DOCUMENT NO: CS SAMPLE

DATE: 15 January, 2003

IDENTIFICATION: Natural Emerald, Colombian*

SHAPE AND CUT: Emerald Cut

CARAT WEIGHT: 3.868 Cts.

MEASUREMENTS: 9.51 x 8.20 x 7.17 mm.

COLOR GRADE: 4 / 70 - 75

Color Rating/Tone   4 / 75

Color Scan G_{70} B_{15} Y_{15}

Light Source   Duro-Test: Vita Lite

CLARITY GRADE: MI_1 - MI_2*

CUTTING GRADE: Very Good (3)
Depth %   61.9%
Brilliancy Range   80 - 100%
Brilliancy Average   80 - 90%

FINISH GRADE: Very Good (3)

NOTE: All color determinations are subject to the color temperature of the light source and the color sensitivity of the observer. The quality and commercial desirability of any color is determined by examining the interrelationships of ALL factors related to Color Grade, including Color Rating, Tone, and Dichroic Effect. Conclusions may vary, within reasonable tolerances, due to the subjective nature of colored stone analysis. Mounted stones are graded only to the extent that mounting permits examination.

COMMENTS: *Total Quality Integration Rating: Excellent. *Based on available gemological information, it is the opinion of the Laboratory that the origin of this material would be classified as Colombia. *It is the opinion of the Laboratory that this material exhibits evidence of faint clarity enhancement (Oil Type Treatment). *Faint texture and dichroic effect [2] present. *The image contained in this document is for representational purposes only and is not necessarily actual color or size. *The conclusions expressed in this report are based on Laboratory determinations effective as of the completion date of this analysis (15 January 2003).

1	2	3	4	5	6	7	8	9	10
Excellent		Very Good		Good		Fair		Poor	

Color Rating (AGL)

0	5	10	15	20	25	30	35	40	45	50	55	60	65	70	75	80	85	90	95	100
V. Light			Light			Light-Med.			Medium					Medium - Dark					Dark - V. Dark	

Tone (AGL) (0 = Colorless, 100 = Black)

FI	LI₁	LI₂	MI₁	MI₂	HI₁	HI₂	EI₁	EI₂
Free of Incl.	Lightly Included		Moderately Included		Highly Included		Excessively Included	

Clarity Scale (AGL)

1	2	3	4	5	6	7	8	9	10
Excellent	Very Good		Good			Fair		Poor	

Cutting / Proportions / Finish (AGL)

This report prepared by:

AGL ™

American Gemological Laboratories, Inc.

© 1978 American Gemological Laboratories, Inc.   Original

American Gemological Laboratories ™   **Colored Stone Grading Report**

580 Fifth Avenue
Suite 706
New York, N.Y. 10036
Tel: (212) 704-0727
Fax: (212) 764-7614

The information contained in this report represents the opinion of American Gemological Laboratories regarding the characteristics of the colored stone(s) submitted for examination.
The conclusions expressed are the American Gemological Laboratories' interpretation of the results obtained from gemological instruments and grading techniques designed for this purpose. Conclusions may vary, within reasonable tolerances, due to the subjective nature of colored stone analysis.

DOCUMENT NO: CS 35230

DATE: 7 December, 2001

IDENTIFICATION: Natural Sapphire, Kashmir*

SHAPE AND CUT: Cushion Antique Mixed Cut

CARAT WEIGHT: Estimated 3.0 Cts.

MEASUREMENTS: 8.15 x 7.28 x 5.77 mm.
(Approximately)

COLOR GRADE: 2.5 / 85*

Color Rating/Tone   2 - 3 / 85

Color Scan B_{75} V_{15} G_{10}

Light Source   Duro-Test: Vita Lite

CLARITY GRADE: LI_2*

CUTTING GRADE: Very Good - Good (3 - 4)
Depth %   79.2%
Brilliancy Range   70 - 100%
Brilliancy Average   80%

FINISH GRADE: Very Good - Good (3 - 4)

NOTE: All color determinations are subject to the color temperature of the light source and the color sensitivity of the observer. The quality and commercial desirability of any color is determined by examining the interrelationships of ALL factors related to Color Grade, including Color Rating, Tone, and Dichroic Effect. Conclusions may vary, within reasonable tolerances, due to the subjective nature of colored stone analysis. Mounted stones are graded only to the extent that mounting permits examination.

COMMENTS: *Total Quality Integration Rating: Excellent - Very Good. *Based on available gemological information, it is the opinion of the Laboratory that the origin of this material would be classified as Kashmir. *Heat Enhancement: None. *Color / Scan Reference: 356 Range. *Faint to moderate color and textural zoning [1], moderate general texture and moderate dichroic effect [2] present. *All information is subject to the limitations imposed by the mounting. *The image contained in this document is for representational purposes only and is not necessarily actual color or size.

1	2	3	4	5	6	7	8	9	10
Excellent		Very Good		Good		Fair		Poor	

Color Rating (AGL)

0	5	10	15	20	25	30	35	40	45	50	55	60	65	70	75	80	85	90	95	100
V. Light			Light			Light-Med.			Medium					Medium - Dark					Dark - V. Dark	

Tone (AGL) (0 = Colorless, 100 = Black)

FI	LI₁	LI₂	MI₁	MI₂	HI₁	HI₂	EI₁	EI₂
Free of Incl.	Lightly Included		Moderately Included		Highly Included		Excessively Included	

Clarity Scale (AGL)

1	2	3	4	5	6	7	8	9	10
Excellent	Very Good		Good			Fair		Poor	

Cutting / Proportions / Finish (AGL)

This report prepared by:

AGL ™

American Gemological Laboratories, Inc.

© 1978 American Gemological Laboratories, Inc.   Original

Bibliography

GEMSTONES
(Alphabetically by type)

Amber

GRIMALDI, DAVID A,, ed., *Amber:Window to the Past.* New York: Harry N. Abrams, 1998.

GÜBELIN, E. J., 'The Tears of The Heliades', *Gems & Gemology* (Gemological Institute of America), Fall 1978.

HUNGER, ROSA, *The Magic of Amber.* Radnor, Pa.: Chilton Book Co., 1979.

RICE, PATTY C., *Amber:The Golden Gem of the Ages.* New York: Van Nostrand Reinhold, 1980.

Diamond

BRUTON, ERIC, *Diamonds.* Ipswich: Eric Bruton Associates, and Radnor, Pa.: Chilton Book Co., 2nd Ed., 1978.

CONTENT, DEREK J., ed., *A Green Diamond.* England: Mayney Press and California: Gemological Institute of America. 1999.

COPELAND, LAWRENCE L., *Diamonds: Famous, Notable and Unique.* GIA, 1974.

EMANUEL, HARRY, *Diamonds and Precious Stones.* London: John Camden Hotren, 1867.

HARLOW, GEORGE E., ed., *The Nature of Diamonds.* Cambridge, U.K.: Cambridge University Press in association with the American Museum of Natural History, 1998.

HOWARTH, STEPHEN, *The Koh-I-Noor Diamond.* London: Quartet Books, 1980.

LENZEN, GODEHARD, *The History of Diamond Production and the Diamond Trade.* London: Barrie & Jenkins, 1970;

—— (Ed.), *Diamonds: Myth, Magic, and Reality.* New York: Crown, 1980.

LEWISOHN, RICHARD, *Barney Barnato.* New York: E. P. Dutton, 1939.

LOCKHART, J. G., and WOODHOUSE, THE HON. C. M., *Rhodes.* London: Hodder and Stoughton, 1963.

NEWTON, CHARLES MANFRED, *A Barrel of Diamonds.* New York: 1980.

TAGORE, SOURINDRO MOHUN, *Mani-Mala, or a Treatise on Gems.* Calcutta, 1879.

WILLIAMS, GARDNER F., *The Diamond Mines of South Africa.* New York: B. F. Buck & Co., 1906.

Emerald

GHEERBRANT, ALAIN, *The Incas: The Royal Commentaries of Garcilaso the Inca.* New York: The Orion Press, 1961.

PAL, PRATAPITYA, ed.., *Romance of the Taj Mahal.* London: Thames & Hudson; Los Angeles: Los Angeles County Museum of Art, 1989.

RAINIER, PETER W., *Green Fire.* London: John Murray, 1943, and New York: 1944.

SINKANKIS, JOHN, *Emerald and other Beryls.* Radnor, Pa.: Chilton Book Co. 1981.

Garnet

AVENT, RICHARD, 'Anglo-Saxon Disc and Composite Brooches', Oxford: *British Archaeological Reports,* 1975.

Beowulf (translated by Charles Kennedy). Oxford University Press, 1968.

J ESSUP, RONALD, *Anglo-Saxon Jewellery.* Princes Risborough: Shire Publications, 1974.

LASZLO, GYULA, *The Art of the Migration Period.* Coral Gables: University of Miami Press, 1974.

Jade

DAVID, SIR PERCIVAL, *Chinese Connoisseurship: The Ko Ku Yao Lun — The Essential Criteria of Antiquities.* London: Faber and Faber, 1971.

GOETTE, JOHN A., *Jade Lore.* Ann Arbor, Mich.: Ars Ceramica, 1976.

GUMP, RICHARD, *Jade, Stone of Heaven.* Garden City, N.Y.: Doubleday, 1962.

HARTMAN, JOAN M., *Chinese Jade Of Five Centuries.*: Rutland, Vt.: Charles E. Tuttle Co., 1966.

KOO, MADAME WELLINGTON, *No Feast Lasts Forever.* New York: Quadrangle/The New York Times Book Co., 1975.

LAUFER, BERTHOLD, *Jade: A Study in Chinese Archeology and Religion.* New York: Dover Publications, 1974.

SCHEDEL, J. J., *The Splendor of Jade: Four Thousand Years of the Art of Jade Carving.* New York: E. P. Dutton, 1974

WATT, JAMES C. Y., *Chinese Jades from Han to Ch'ing.* New York: The Asia Society, 1980.

Lapis

HERMANN, GEORGINA, "Lapis Lazuli: The Early Phases of Its Trade," In *Iraq Magazine.* From Ph.D. Thesis, "The Source, Distribution, History and Use of Lapis Lazuli in Western Asia from the Earliest Times to the End of the Seleucid Era." Oxford University, 1966.

MAXWELL-HYSLOP, K. R., *Western Asiatic Jewellery, C. 3000–612 B.C.* London: Methuen, 1970.

Opal

EYLES, WILFRED CHARLES, *The Book of Opals.* Rutland, Vt.: Charles E. Tuttle Co., 1976.

KALOKERINOS, ARCHIE, *In Search of Opal.* Sydney: Ure Smith, 1967.

LEECHMAN, FRANK, *The Opal Book.* Sydney: Ure Smith, 1961.

O'LEARY, BARRIE, *A Field Guide to Australian Opals.* Norwood, South Australia: Rigby, 1977.

Pearl

CONTENT, DEREK J., ed., *The Pearl and the Dragon: A Study of Vietnamese Pearls and a History of the Oriental Pearl Trade.* Houlton, Maine: Derek J. Content, et al, with the cooperation of The Gemological Institute of America, 1999.

DICKINSON, J., *The Book of Pearls.* New York: Crown, 1968.

EUNSON, ROBERT, *The Pearl King: The Story of the Fabulous Mikimoto.* London: Angus And Robertson, 1956.

REECE, NORINE C., *The Cultured Pearl: Jewel of Japan.* Rutland, Vt.: Charles E. Tuttle Co., 1970.

ROSENTHAL, LEONARD, *The Pearl Hunter.* New York: Henry Schuman, 1952.

SHIRAI, SHOHEI, *The Story of Pearls.* Tokyo: Japan Publications, 1970.

Ruby

CLAUDET, ARTHUR C. (Ed.), *Transactions of the Institution of Mining & Metallurgy,* Vol. 5, London.

TAVERNIER, JEAN-BAPTISTE, *The Six Voyages of Jean-Baptiste Tavernier, Baron of Aubonne, Through Turk[e]y into Persia and the East Indies [error for India] for the Space of Forty Years. . . .* (translated by John Phillips). London: Dr. Daniel Cox, 1676.

Sapphire

GÜBELIN, F. J., *The Internal World of Gemstones.* Zurich: ABC Edition, 1974. (*see* chapter on Sapphires.)

Turquoise

BENNET, EDNA MAE, *Turquoise and the Indians.* Chicago: The Swallow Press, 1970.

FRAZIER, GLORIA, *Navajos Call it Hard Goods.* 1976. Gloria Frazier, P.O. Box 18242, Tucson, Arizona 85731.

LAUFER, BERTHOLD, *Notes on Turquois in the East.* Chicago: Field Museum of Natural History, July 1913.

POGUE, JOSEPH F., *Turquoise: Memoirs of the National Academy of Sciences.* Glorieta (New Mexico): The Rio Grande Press, 1975.

ROSNEK, CARL, AND STACEY, JOSEPH, *Sky-Stone and Silver: The Collector's Book of South West Indian Jewelry.* Englewood Cliffs, N.J.: Prentice-Hall, 1976.

GEMOLOGY

ANDERSON, B. W., *Gemstones for Everyman.* London: Faber And Faber, 1976.

AREM, JOEL E., *Man-Made Crystals.* Washington, D.C.: Smithsonian Institution Press, 1973.

BANK, HERMAN, *From The World of Gemstones.* Innsbruck: Pinguin-Verlag, 1973.

DESAUTELS, PAUL E., *Gems in the Smithsonian Museum.* Washington, D.C.: Smithsonian Institution Press, 1972;

———, *The Mineral Kingdom.* New York: Grosset & Dunlap, 1974;

———, *The Gem Collection.* Washington, D.C.: Smithsonian Institution Press, 1979.

GÜBELIN, E. J., *The Internal World of Gemstones.* Zurich: ABC Edition, 1974.

LIDDICOAT, RICHARD T., JR., *Handbook of Gem Identification.* Santa Monica, Cal.: Gemological Institute of America. 1977.

NASSAU, KURT, *Gems Made By Man.* Radnor, Pa.: Chilton Book Co., 1980.

SAUER, JULES ROGER, *Brazil: Paradise of Gemstones.* Rio De Janeiro, Aggs Press, 1982.

SCHUBNEL, HENRI-JEAN, *Pierres Precieuses Dans Le Monde.* Paris: Horizons De France, 1968.

SINKANKIS, JOHN, *Gemstone & Mineral Data Book.* New York: Winchester Press, 1972.

VARLEY, HELEN (Ed.), *Color.* Los Angeles: The Knapp Press, 1980.

WALCH, MARGARET, *Color Source Book.* New York: Charles Scribner's Sons, 1971.

WEBSTER, ROBERT, *Gems: Their Sources, Descriptions, and Identification.* London: Butrerworth, and Hamden, Conn.: Shoestring Press, 4th rev. ed. 1983.

GEMS, ECONOMICS AND LITERATURE

ANNUAL REPORTS: De Beers Consolidated Mines Limited Annual Reports, 36 Stock-Dale St., Kimberley, South Africa.

GREGORY, SIR THEODORE, *Ernest Oppenheimer And The Economic Development Of Southern Africa.* London: Oxford University Press, 1962.

LEVITT, ARTHUR, JR., *How to Make Your Money Make Money.* Homewood, Ill.: Dow Jones-Irwin, 1981.

MOYERSOEN, JEAN-FRANÇOIS, *Investing In Diamonds.* New York: Gem Reports, a Division of John Wolf Publications, 1980.

ZUCKER, BENJAMIN, *How to Invest in Gems: Everyone's Guide to Buying Rubies, Sapphires, Emeralds & Diamonds.* New York: Quadrangle/The New York Times Book Co., 1976; and 2nd ed. published as *How to Buy & Sell Gems: Everyone's Guide to Rubies, Sapphires, Emeralds & Diamonds.* New York: Quadrangle/The New York Times Book Co., 1979 (reprinted 1984); Also French Edition, *Acheter Des Pierres Précieuses: Pourquoi–Quand–Comment* (translated and adapted by B. Süssmann). Geneva: Editions Hugo Buchser Sa., 1981; and Hebrew Edition, **איך להשקיע באבני־חן**. Tel Aviv: Editions Sadan, 1980. *Blue: A Novel.* Woodstock & New York: The Overlook Press, 2000; *Green: A Novel.* Woodstock & New York: The Overlook Press, 2002.

THE HISTORY AND TECHNIQUES OF JEWELRY MAKING

ALDRED, CYRIL, *Jewels of the Pharaohs.* London: Thames and Hudson, and New York: Ballantine Books, 1979.

ARWAS, V., *Art Deco.* London: Academy Editions, 1980.

BALL, SIDNEY H., *Historical Notes on Gem Mining,* 1931.

BATTKE, H., *Geschichte des Ringes in Beschreibung und Bildern.* Baden-Baden, 1953.

BERLIN, B., AND KAY, P., *Basic Color Terms: Their Universality and Evolution.* University of California Press, 1969 (U.S.A.) and 1970 (U.K.).

BLACK, J. ANDERSON, *The Story of Jewelry.* New York: William Morrow, 1974.

BRADFORD, ERNIE, *Four Centuries of European Jewelry.* London: Spring Books, 1967.

CELIINI, BENVENUTO: *The Treatises of Benvenuto Cellini in Goldsmithing and Sculpture* (trans. C. R. Ashbee). London: Guild of Handicraft, 1898.

Cheapside Hoard of Elizabethan and Jacobean Jewellery, The. London Museum Catalogue No. 2, 1928.

COARELLI, FILIPPO, *Greek and Roman Jewellery.* London: Hamlyn, 1970.

EVANS, JOAN, *Magi Cal Jewels of the Middle Ages and Renaissance, Particularly in England.* Oxford: The Clarendon Press, 1922;

—— *English Posies and Posy Rings.* London: Oxford University Press, 1931; *A History of Jewellery, 1100-1870* (rev. ed.). London: Faber and Faber, and Boston, Mass.: Boston Book and Art, 1970.

FALK, F. 'Edelsteinschliff und Fassungsformen im Späten Mittelalter und im 16. Jahrhundert: Studium Zur Geschichte Der Edelstein und des Schmuckes.' Thesis, Tübingen University, 1973.

FRÉGNAC, CLAUDE, *Jewellery. from the Renaissance to Art Nouveau.* London: Weidenfeld and Nicolson, 1966.

GANS, M. H., *Juwelen En Mensen.* Schiedam, The Netherlands: Interbook International, 1979.

GRAHAM-CAMPBELL, JAMES, *Viking Artefacts: A Select Catalogue.* London: British Museum Publications, 1980.

GREGORIETTI, GUIDO, *Jewelry Through the Ages.* New York: American Heritage, 1969, and London: Hamlyn, 1970.

HACKENBROCH, YVONNE, *Renaissance Jewellery.* London and Totowa, N.J.: Philip Wilson Publishers Ltd for Sotheby Parke Bernet Publications, 1980.

HENIG, M., "A Corpus of Roman Engraved Gemstones from British Sites." Oxford: *British Archaeological Reports,* 1974.

HIGGINS, R. A., *Greek and Roman Jewellery.* London: Methuen, 1961, 1981.

HUGHES, GRAHAM, *Modern Jewelry. An International Survey 1890-1963.* New York and London: Studio Books, 1963;

——, *The Art of Jewelry.* New York: Viking Press, and London: Studio Vista, 1972.

LANLLIER, JEAN, AND PINI, MARIE-ANNE, *Cinq Siècles de Joaillerie en Occident.* Fribourg: Office Du Livre, 1971.

LASZLO, GYULA, *The Art of the Migration Period.* Coral Gables, Fla.: University of Miami Press, 1974.

MASON, ANITA, AND PACKER, DIANE, *An Illustrated Dictionary of Jewellery*. Reading: Osprey Publishing, 1973, and New York: Harper & Row, 1974.

MAXWELL-HYSLOP, K. R., *Western Asiatic Jewellery, C. 3000-612 B.C.* London: Methuen, 1970.

MULLER, PRISCILLA E., *Jewels iIn Spain, 1500-1800*. New York: Hispanic Society of America, 1972.

NEWMAN, HAROLD, *An Illustrated Dictionary of Jewelry*. London and New York: Thames And Hudson, 1981.

OMAN, C. C., *British Rings, 800-1914*. London: Batsford, 1974.

PARROT, A., *Sumer*. London: Thames and Hudson, 1960.

RUDOE, JUDY, *Cartier, 1900–1939*. London: British Museum Press, 1997.

SCARISBRICK, DIANA, *Chaumet: Master Jewellers since 1780*. Paris: Alain de Gourcuff, 1995.

———, *Jewellery in Britain, 1006–1937: A Documentary, Social, Literary and Artistic Survey*. Wilby, Norwich: Michael Russell, 1944.

———, *Tudor and Jacobean Jewellery*. London: Tate Publishing, 1995.

SCARISBRICK, DIANA (ed.), *Livre D'aneaux De Pierre Woeiriot*. Oxford: Ashmolean Museum, 1978.

STEINGRÄBER, E., *Antique Jewellery. Its History in Europe From 800 to 1900*. London: Thames and Hudson, 1957.

TAVERNIER, JEAN-BAPTISTE, *The Six Voyages of Jean-Baptiste Tavernier, Baron of Aubonne, Through Turk[e]y into Persia and The East Indies [error for India] for the Space of Forty Years*. (Translated By John Phillips). London: Dr. Daniel Cox, 1676.

TAYLOR, GERALD, AND SCARISBRICK, DIANA, *Finger Rings: From Ancient Egypt to the Present Day*. London: Lund Humphries, 1978.

TWINING, LORD, *A History of the Crown Jewels of Europe*. London: Batsford, 1960.

UNTRACHT, OPPI, *Metal Techniques for Craftsmen*. Garden City, N.Y.: Doubleday, 1968.

VEVER, H., *La Bijouterie Française au Xixe Siècle*. Paris: 1906, 1908.

VILIMKOVA, MILADA, *Egyptian Jewellery*. London: Hamlyn, 1969.

WARD, ANNE, CHERRY, JOHN, GERE, CHARLOTTE, and CARTIIDGE, BARBARA, *The Ring from Antiquity to the Twentieth Century*. London: Thames and Hudson, and New York: Rizzoli, 1981.

WULFF, HANS E., *The Traditional Crafts of Persia*. Cambridge, Mass.: M.I.T. Press, 1966.

CATALOGS

Jewelry Collections:

Catalogue of Finger Rings: Early Christian, Byzantine, Teutonic, Medieval and Later. Bequeathed by Sir Augustus Franks by O. M. Dalton. London: British Museum, 1912.

Catalogue of Rings by C. C. Oman. London: Victoria And Albert Museum, 1930.

Superb Collection of Rings [of G. Guilhou, of Paris]. London: Sotheby & Co., 1937.

The Melvin Gutman Jewelry. New York: Parke Bernet Galleries, 1969.

The Ralph Harari Collection of Finger Rings by John Boardman and Diana Scarisbrick. London: Thames and Hudson, 1978.

Jewelry Exhibitions:

Finger Rings from Ancient Egypt to the Present Day. Oxford: Ashmolean Museum, 1978.

Jewellery Through 7000 Years. London: British Museum, 1976.

Jewelry: Ancient to Modern. Baltimore, Md.: Walters Art Gallery, 1979. Also New York: Viking Press, 1980.

Princely Magnificence: Court Jewels of the Renaissance, 1500-1630. London: Victoria And Albert Museum, 1980.

Romance of the Taj Mahal. Lost Angeles: Los Angeles County Museum, 1989.

Acknowledgments

I am deeply indebted to my father, Charles Zucker. He predicted that, in the writing of a book about gems and jewels, I would eventually write novels as well. As in so many things, his vision came to be.

Rachel Zucker reviewed the text with a poet's touch and a photographer's eye.

I'd like to thank Miranda Leigh Pildes, who combined historical and gemological expertise to adapt and update the third edition of this book.

All at The Overlook Press made working on this new edition a great pleasure: Peter Mayer's enthusiasm, the editorial work of Caroline Trefler, and once again Bernard Schleifer's "miraculous eye" has meant so much to me

I greatly appreciate Ricki Borger for her enthusiastic and discerning love of jewelry. Having friends abroad helped to give me a wide perspective. Conversations with the Kan family and the guidance of Victor Klagsbald were very important to me.

Several eminent figures in the gemological world were especially helpful. Dr, Eduard Gübelin was gracious in his reading and advice, as were Bob Crowningshield, Tom Moses, Kenneth Scarrett, Ralph Esmerian, Henri Masliah, Ronnie Roubin, Luzer Kaufman, Cap Beesley, Bernard and Peggy Grosz, Jesse Wolfgang, and Albert and Harry Kleinhaus.My fellow dealers in colored stones have been uniformly helpful, as have been so many others in the diamond world. I thank Jan Mitchell for his aesthetic inspiration, and Bethsabée and Roland Sussmann, who were both instrumental in the preparation of the book.

For me, the loveliness of gems has been clarified in conversations with my friends Samuel and Laurel Beizer, Derek Content, John Flattau, Daniel Friedenberg, Milton Moses Ginsberg, David Jaffe, Michael and Elizabeth Varet, Bernie Zucker, Bill Gross, Jeanne and Alfred Moldovan and Bob Gray. Diana Scarisbrick and the entire Norton family have patiently shared with me their connoisseur's eye for the beautiful in jewelry.

Memories of the love of Lotty Zucker and Nikki Zucker echo through these pages. The encouragement of Margot Zucker Mindich and Lenny Mindich are much appreciated. Finally, it is to Barbara—in an age of fiberglass, very much a gem— I give my deepest thanks.

CHAPTER ACKNOWLEDGMENTS

1. RUBY
My thanks go to the remarkable Professor Harry Bober and to the Sri Lanka State Gem Corporation, for their help.

2. SAPPHIRE
I thank Geoffrey Munn for his generous help, and Dr. Alfred Moldovan for providing inspiration. The Sri Lanka State Gem Corporation aided me by providing information and tours of relatively inaccessible mining areas. Stories about gems were recounted to me by Diane Wolkstein, and to her I give my thanks.

3. EMERALD
I wish to thank fellow gem dealers for their help in preparing this text. Also, I am much indebted to Diana Scarisbrick for her encouragement.

4. WHITE DIAMOND
I thank De Deers consolidated mines limited for their unfailing courtesy and help. My thanks also go to Willi Nagel, Tony Nagel, and Adam Nagel. The staff of the Gemological Institute of America, Louis Glick, Simon Glick, Albert and Harry

Kleinhaus, Dr. Eduard Gübelin, Cap Beesley, Dennis Scioli, Gary Schuler, Francois Curiel, Simon Teakle, Dennis Scioli, Gary Schuler, Jesse Wolfgang, Albert and Raphael Haberkorn, and, finally, other diamond dealers who aided me greatly but preferred to remain anonymous.

5. COLORED DIAMOND
I would like to thank the staff of the Gemological Institute of America for their assistance. De Beers, Lewis Beck, Tom Moses, the Doppelt Brothers, Marcus Fuchs, were all exceptionally generous with guidance and time.

6. PEARL
I thank my father, Charles Zucker, and Luzer Kaufman for their help in explaining to me both the beauty of pearl and the intricacies of the market. I am grateful to Henri Masliah for his help. The Mikimoto Company was extraordinarily generous with advice, photographs and guidance; and, of course, Kan Yue and the entire Kan family—with his extraordinary knowledge of pearls and gems —was invaluable to me. Kenneth Scarratt, as well as Derek J. Content, James Traub, Georges Ruiz, (as well as the editorial skills of Rachel Zucker), made the research on the royal Vietnamese pearl collection a great pleasure

7. AMBER
Wolf Hunger of Sac Frères introduced me to the beauty of amber; his great knowledge and courtesy are much appreciated. Derek Content, Jack Ogden and Geoffrey Munn were particularly generous in advising on the historical aspects of amber. The Sac Frères pieces illustrated were photographed by Peter Schaaf.

8. LAPIS
Diane Wolksrein, in *Inanna, Queen of Heaven and Earth — her stories and hymns fromSsumer* (Harper & Row, 1982), revealed to me the metaphysical beauty of lapis. The Schaffer family of A La Vieille Russie have been most courteous to me and graciously helpful, and Professor Harry Bober's enthusiasm and patient help are much appreciated.

9. JADE
This chapter was made possible only because of the extensive help and time I received from members of the Asia Society. Dr. James C. Y. Watt's superb catalogue, *Chinese Jade from Han to Ch'ing*, aided me very

much, as did Mahrukh Tarapor's guide to the jade exhibition. Information, photos and education were all provided to me in a generous fashion. Information on jade carving in china today was provided by the Tianjin Arts and Crafts Board, which allowed me to tour a jade factory, to see at first hand the continuity of Chinese skill in fashioning jade. Finally, Bert Krashes of the Gemological Institute of America provided me with help and inspiration through his lectures on jade.

10. TURQUOISE
I thank the general staff at the Museum of the American Indian in New York—especially Barbara Christ and Carmelo Guadagno (the photographer)—and the curatorial staff, who were extraordinarily helpful to me.

11. OPAL
John Cubitto's photos and guidance, as well as the gemological guidance of Cap Beesley are very much appreciated.

12. GARNET
I offer my thanks to Jack Ogden and Derek Content for their continuous help in unravelling the mysteries of ancient and medieval jewelry. The quotation from *Beowulf* on p. 223 is reprinted by permission of Oxford University Press.

PICTURE CREDITS

The author and publisher wish to thank the following for their courtesy in supplying photographs and for permitting their use in this book:

A La Vieille Russie, New York 76, 177, 179
American Gemological Laboratories, Inc. 27-29, 31-4, 60
The American Museum of Natural History, New York 6, 58, 108
Ares Antiques Gallery, New York 180, 229
The Asia Society, New York 192
Assael International 148
Bei Shan Tang Collection 186
Professor Harry Bober 173
Connie Brauer, Denver 230, 231
Brighton Museum, Sussex 156
Trustees of the British Museum 168, 170, 213, 243, 245, 246, 251
Cartier, Paris 20
Chaumet, Paris 102, 117